IS BARBA

After reading her essays or seeing her perform, people sang her praises (and she didn't have to pay them much, either)

Barbara was fantastic! Brilliant, insightful, playful, self-deprecating, and we could all relate.
—Lois P.

I felt she was speaking just to me.
—Louise W.

Great presentation—lots of laffs. She rocked the house!
—Betsy G.

LOL—I love this spoof on designer Thanksgiving food orders. . . .God bless you, Barbara, and next year do pot luck. Thanks for making me smile.
—Emily G.

All I can say is WOW! Barbara was absolutely terrific, funny, articulate, and pitch-perfect. We loved it!
—Steve H.

She was amazing. Absolutely fabulous. I had a great time.
—Maxine P.

If there had been a People's Choice Award, she would have won it.

                                       –Gary D.

The needle couldn't go high enough on the applause meter!

                                       –Diane Z.

Thanks for the Christmas chuckles, Barbara. I felt like I was there.

                                       –Julie L.

She brought down the house.

                                       –Tony M.

Can I have your autograph?

                                       –Adele R.

When Barbara addressed the GaGa Sisterhood, she had us all in stitches with her self-deprecating humor. From the miseries of thinning hair and shrinking height to the mysteries of our grown kids' employment, Barbara seems to read the minds of people 'of a certain age' and turn their cause for concern into cause for laughter."

        –Donne Davis, founder and director of
          GaGa Sisterhood and author of
          When Being a Grandma Isn't So Grand

THIS OLD BODY

Thanks for laughing
along with me!
Barbara

BOOKS BY BARBARA GREENLEAF

*THIS OLD BODY: And 99 Other Reasons
to Laugh at Life*

*HELP: A Handbook for Working Mothers
with Louis Schaffer, M.D.*

Children Through the Ages: A History of Childhood

America Fever: The Story of American Immigration

Young Adult Novels

Good-to-Go Café

Animal Kingdom

Juvenile Biography

*Forward March to Freedom:
A Biography of A. Philip Randolph*

THIS
OLD BODY

AND 99 OTHER REASONS
TO LAUGH AT LIFE

Barbara Greenleaf

More Mesa Press

Published by

More Mesa Press
Post Office Box 610
Goleta, CA 93116

ISBN: (paperback) 978-1-64570-405-8
ISBN: (ebook) 978-1-64570-406-5

For more information, group sales, and booking
Barbara for your next event:
Barbara@barbaragreenleaf.com

This is a creative work drawn from life. Any
resemblance to random individuals, living or dead,
portrayed in the book is purely coincidental.

Cartoon licensed from
Condé Nast-The Cartoon Bank
Cover photograph: Jon Greenleaf

Printed in the United States of America

For my chiropractor, nutritionist, physical therapist, dermatologist, Pilates instructor, acupuncturist, massage technician, hairdresser, and everyone else who props up this old body

"I used to be old, too, but it wasn't my cup of tea."

CONTENTS

PART TWO
MARRIED SINCE THE FIRST CRUSADE

CONTENTS

PART THREE
MUDDLING THROUGH MODERN LIFE

INTRODUCTION

When humor goes, there goes civilization.
—Erma Bombeck

As people of a certain age, we're all familiar with that classic TV show, "This Old House." But I always thought PBS would get even more viewers with a series called, "This Old Body." So, although nobody asked me, I took it upon myself to put together a series of personal essays, poems, and jokes that highlight the lowlights of aging. In my not-so-humble opinion, any one of them could be the basis for a TV episode.

Thinking along these lines represents a big change for me. Until recently I was always very serious in my work as a historian, author, and blogger. I was not even remotely what the old Hollywood publicists called a "laff riot." But as I got older, I got funnier (decrepitude can do that to you, you know). The folks at *BoomerCafe.com* started publishing my humorous personal essays, then organizations started asking me to read them, and pretty soon I was specializing in the funny side of aging (the last stage before senility sets in, no doubt).

I hope you will laugh along with me at our changing bodies, the ridiculousness of middle-aged love, and the annoyances of modern life (or is it the annoyances of middle-aged love and the ridiculousness of modern life?). If nothing else, it's good for your health. I just read that people who laughed often—thus freeing up all those feel-good endorphins—had 66% lower levels of inflammation than people who didn't laugh much. For that reason alone, we might as well give it a go...

Cheers!

Barbara

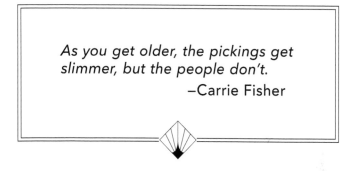

As you get older, the pickings get slimmer, but the people don't.
—Carrie Fisher

PART ONE

AGING: WHY DIDN'T ANYBODY WARN ME?

HAIR: THE REALITY NOT THE MUSICAL

I always liked my hair: It was thick and wavy and adapted easily to every style that was in. But, basically, like teeth until they ache or heels until they blister, hair—until it falls out—is something one simply takes for granted. Recently mine has been falling out or, as the euphemism goes, "thinning."

From time to time I thought my hair looked a little sparse on top, but I didn't really pay attention to it until that night at dinner when my husband happened to glance at my head as I bent over to cut into a lamb chop. "My God, you have a bald spot!" he blurted out. When he saw my stricken expression, he said casually, "Oh, it's only a tiny one; no one will notice."

That was it: I could no longer ignore the signs of imminent balding. Was it my imagination or was I suddenly growing a high forehead? I wrung my hands over every strand that remained in my comb and every wisp that fell into the sink. I began to look at ads for wigs and experimented with concealing styles. In fact, playing with my fast-diminishing locks became a major activity. I changed my part to the left side since the thinning seemed most notice-able on the right, all the while telling myself that this was *not* a comb-over. (Right.) I also tried criss-crossing the top layers. Good for Raggedy Ann, not so good for me. Finally, I sprayed brown colorizer on my scalp to make it look like hair, the way a homeowner would spray green paint on his concrete yard to make it look like grass.

These tactics, of course, were merely cosmetic. It was time to get to the root of the problem (you should pardon the pun). Since desperate times call for desperate measures, I made an appointment with a dermatologist, who prescribed Women's Rogaine. The instructions say you not only have to rub this foamy substance into your scalp EVERY DAY, you can never stop or your hair will fall out again. Oh, and there is one other teensy-weensy downside: you might grow unwanted hair in places other than your head. Great. Now, not only would my husband and I have matching bald spots, we'd have matching his and hers mustaches, too.

Undaunted, I started using the Rogaine, but my efforts didn't stop there. I also got a laser comb, which I was supposed to frog walk over my scalp a quarter inch at a time, three times a week. That did not sound too onerous, but it did sound mind numbing. To counteract the boredom and get in a little exercise, too, I began to multi-task by standing on one leg for balance, squeezing a hand-gripper for strength, and climbing up and down steps for endurance. Occasionally, I would go through the mail. Beeeeep, beeeep . . .

I've only been in the hair-growth game for five weeks and I've been told not to expect signs of progress for at least three to six months. Still, each night I search hopefully for the little row of fuzz that will signal a return to the old me. Hair. This woman's crowning glory, indeed!

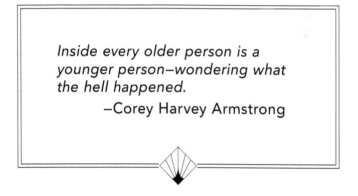

Inside every older person is a younger person—wondering what the hell happened.

         –Corey Harvey Armstrong

WHAT AM I DOING HERE?

When I ask, "What am I doing here?", I don't mean it in the existential sense of "What's man's purpose on earth?", I mean it in the literal sense of "Why the hell did I walk into this room and what exactly am I supposed to be looking for?" Deep thinkers have always pondered the big picture, but right now I would prefer help with the little picture, such as where I dropped my keys or what's the name of the person who sat next to me at last night's dinner party and what did I promise to email him? In other words, what can I do about the everyday memory lapses that are driving me crazy? In his book *Moonwalking with Einstein*, author Jonathan Foer tells us we are what we remember. If that's the case, I'm shedding weight fast.

Foer also tells us that the ancient Greek philosopher Socrates warned against writing because it would "create forgetfulness in the learner's soul." He should only know. Between cell phones, tablets, and artificial intelligence, we now have so many technological crutches we practically have to check with Siri or Alexa to remember our own name. We Boomers blame memory loss on our age. Say *I'm having a senior moment* as you fumfer around for a word, and your pals chuckle knowingly. But when all you ordered at a café was a diet Coke and the young waiter has to return to your table to inquire if that Coke was diet or regular, you know our whole society's in trouble.

Still, we soldier on. Some people use the Greeks' original system in which you picture a house and put a thought in each room (which gave us the phrases "in the first place" and "in the second place.") Others try to repeat a new acquaintance's name or rhyme it with one of her attributes, such as *Sweet Sue in a dress so blue*. Okay, that's pretty easy, but what happens when you meet Walter, who has hair growing out of his ear like a forest? I can see rhyming *stare* and *hair*, but *Walter*? not so much. Some people make up a nonsense sentence that includes everything on their to-do list. And when it comes to remembering numbers, others attach a thought to them. If a code is 4925, for example, they would think of a May-December romance in which the man is middle aged and the girlfriend is a chick. Let's face it, though, these mnemonic devices are time-consuming, mentally exhausting, and only marginally effective because you've still got to remember them, which brings us back to my original dilemma.

Let's concentrate, people! Lest we forget, I'm still wandering aimlessly around my bedroom. Am I here to take a nap, pull a scarf from the dresser, rub cream on my hands, or pick up the landline? It's anybody's guess. So, let's just keep this little incident between the two of us. I'm going to tiptoe backwards out of the room now and pretend it never happened—in the first place.

LONG-TERM COMMITMENT

Recent widow who has just buried fourth husband. Looking for someone to round out a six-unit plot. Dizziness, fainting, shortness of breath not a problem.

—Florida retirement complex ad

BEDTIME—AT LAST!

Among the many things we lose as we age is the ability to flop into bed and just conk out. When I was young I donned my PJ's, brushed my teeth, found the pillow, and was gone. There were no elaborate relaxation routines, no beauty rituals, and certainly no Ambien required to fall asleep. But now in middle age, going to bed entails so many steps that I practically have to start my routine right after dinner to get them all in.

I begin with a bath. I light a candle, plug in the aromatherapy machine, and lower myself into steaming water armed with a crossword puzzle, my Kindle, and an online Scrabble app. I don't let the water out until I'm prune-like (and if I haven't gotten 22-across, I will remain shivering in an empty tub until I do). Upon toweling off, there's the electric toothbrush, the waxed Glide dental floss (My dentist says, "Ignore your teeth and they'll go away"), and minty mouthwash. After that come the eye drops, anti-inflammatories, and bone health pills not to mention a slew of Vitamins from A to Z.

With all of that out of the way, I have to make some decisions. Sleep aid: Should I take the one that knocks me out but only lasts four hours or the one that doesn't knock me out but keeps me in the twilight zone longer? Socks: Put them on to warm my feet now or take them off so I won't feel hot later? Ditto, the extra blanket. Then there's the fan: On or off, high, medium or low? Window: Shut it tight or leave it open? (Dr. Weill admonishes, "Fresh air is a known sleep aid.") Midnight snack? (Conflicting advice: "People sleep better on a full stomach" versus "If you eat anything after 7 pm, you're going to gain weight.").

Next up are the face cream, lip cream and eye cream.

Husband: *"Isn't it time you gave that up, already?"*

Me: *"Probably, but if I do, I'll just lie awake all night imagining my skin crumpling into wrinkles like used tissue paper."*

Finally, I'm into the home stretch:

1) Turn alarm clock toward the wall (The magazine gurus advise, "Be sure to cover all glaring electronic devices").

2) Get rid of reading matter ("Only use the bed for sex or sleeping").

3) Cling to edge of bed lest I inadvertently roll across the invisible center line onto husband's side, a boundary more closely guarded (and hotly contested) than Korea's 38th parallel.

4) Place head on environmentally sound bamboo pillow.

5) Hope for the best.

I accept that the glory days of deep REM sleep may be behind me, but is more than four hours out of the question? If so, I'll know for certain that I've turned into my grandfather, who used to prowl the halls in the predawn hours. When I, too, start having breakfast at 5:30 a.m., I'll know the true meaning of the phrase, "Early Bird Special."

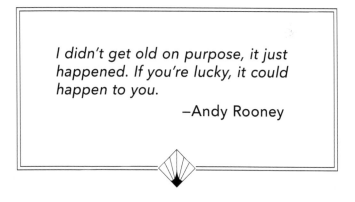

I didn't get old on purpose, it just happened. If you're lucky, it could happen to you.

—Andy Rooney

COMING INTO FOCUS

I've worn glasses since I was seven years old. You name the shape (oval, square, rectangular), the color (red, black, tortoise shell, gunmetal), or the pattern (checked, speckled, glen plaid)—if they made 'em, I wore 'em. Then a funny thing happened on the way to middle age, I had cataract surgery.

Doctors today insist that it's up to the patient to determine when he/she is ready for the operation. Some people say "when" if they see auras around headlights at night, or everything is blurry in one eye, or they have to memorize the eye chart before going to the DMV. For me the moment of truth came at Dunkin' Donuts. I couldn't read the labels on the bins too clearly, so, although what I wanted was a glazed donut, what I ordered was an apple cruller. After this shocking turn of events, I immediately made a beeline for the ophthalmologist's.

I had my cataracts removed and things are brighter now, but it's been an adjustment. For starters, wrinkles that I never saw before suddenly loomed larger than the San Andreas Fault. And with the removal of eyeglasses, a multitude of sins they had hidden were suddenly there for all to see: bags, frown lines, crow's feet, and unplucked eyebrows.

Another downside has been the "cheaters" dilemma. I never had to look for my glasses before because they were always on my nose. Now, like so much else in middle age, my new reading glasses require a strategy. Some people my age buy a gross from the drugstore and stash one in every room, in their car, in their purses, and in their pockets. Others wear them on a chain around their neck, and still others push them up on their forehead. I can't seem to come up with a satisfactory system. I walk out of a room with glasses shoved into my shirt, then wonder where they are. I take them into a restaurant, read the menu, and leave them on the table. I sometimes forget to pack them altogether when I go to a concert. Then I have to ask my neighbor, is the next number a tribute to Mozart or Mongo Santamaria?

A victim of my times, I used to stumble around when I went on a date in order to look attractive, thinking, as the humorist Dorothy Parker famously observed, "Men don't make passes at girls who wear glasses." This piece of settled wisdom was reinforced by the romance comic books of my youth. In them when a woman found the man of her dreams, she threw caution—and her specs—to the wind as she was swept off her feet by Mr. Adorable. I always wondered where she literally went from there? Too late for me, glasses are now a major fashion statement, that is if you can wheel your suitcase full of reading specs, computer specs, distance specs, and sunglasses around with you.

On the upside, I can now see which way I'm going in the pool, try hairstyles that were out of bounds before (although I may be a little old for dreadlocks), and wear long earrings, which I always thought looked weird with glasses. Yes, cataract removal was a miracle operation, but let it also be said there are times when you have to be careful what you wish for.

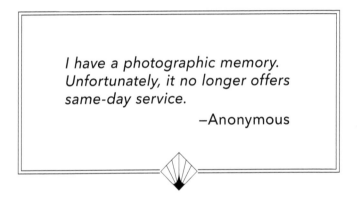

*I have a photographic memory.
Unfortunately, it no longer offers
same-day service.*

—Anonymous

THE ELDERLY SHOULD STAY INDOORS

There's always an "aha!" moment when people realize they've moved up into the next age bracket. For some it's qualifying for a senior discount at the movies. For others it's perusing the 55+ menu at Denny's. For still others it's being called "Mr." or "Mrs.," to which many reply in indignation, "Call me Stan. Mr. Whitaker is my father." For me it was the announcement during a heat wave that the elderly should stay indoors. My first thought was, "That's so nice. Our mayor really cares about her senior citizens." My second thought was, "My God, she's talking to me!"

Who doesn't go kicking and screaming into that dreaded category, "the elderly?" It has so many connotations, all of them negative, and it doesn't square with our image of ourselves as vibrant, attractive, fully functioning members of society. Inwardly and often outwardly we vigorously protest that yes, age-wise, we may qualify for Social Security, but in every other way we're not like the rest of *them*. I love the New Yorker cartoon in the front of this book in which a woman in an outlandish mod outfit tells the frump standing next to her, "I used to be old, too. But it wasn't my cup of tea." It isn't my cup of tea, either, but here I am, nonetheless.

With the realization that I had gotten into this new category and wasn't getting out came a whole host of other acknowledgements. The U.S. Government was never going to put my face on a postage stamp—or a Wanted poster, either. I was never going to have a highway named after me. (Each day when I drive over the freeway I wonder who was that Sgt. Randolph Titus, anyway, and what did he do to merit an overpass?). I have accepted that I'll never be a female "first," as in the first woman to fly solo over the Atlantic (darn that Amelia Earhart) or win the Nobel Prize in chemistry (not to be petty, but Marie Curie did have a lot of help from Pierre), or swim the English Channel (although those in the know say my butterfly stroke is truly awesome).

My husband always protests that his grandparents were old, we're not old. Oh, no? Then how come we wake up each morning eager to discover the ailment du jour: Will it be leg cramp, trigger finger, lower back pain, frozen shoulder, or trick knee? At least we're still active, we reassure ourselves, albeit with a little help from our friends such as Aleve. Sixty is the new forty we're told, yet I don't notice any forty-somethings rushing to trade places with us.

Hopefully, I'll be among the "elderly" for a long time, so I'm making my peace with it. I'm trying to give myself credit for what I've accomplished and forgive myself for what I haven't. As one ancient Chinese artist wrote, "I drew the best line I could that day." And, lo and behold, I'm still dipping my pen into the inkwell.

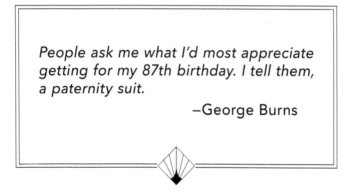

People ask me what I'd most appreciate getting for my 87th birthday. I tell them, a paternity suit.

–George Burns

TAI CHI AND ME

When I gather the clouds in my hands
And thrust up my arms to open
The gates of heaven
I hear the lawnmower start up at the
    Browns' next door.

And when I clutch the tiger to my breast
And breathe in mindfully through my nose
And let out evil spirits through my mouth
I'm pondering if my coupon from Sears is
    still any good.

And when I soulfully combine yin and yang
And sink organically into the earth
While gracefully forming the tai chi basket
    with my palms
I'm wondering if my appointment's at the
    ophthalmologist or the gynecologist.

AGING: WHY DIDN'T ANYBODY WARN ME?

Yes, the tinkle of temple bells summons
My soul to an exalted place
But until I'm received there in my saffron
    robes
When are the Browns going to shut off that
    damn lawnmower!

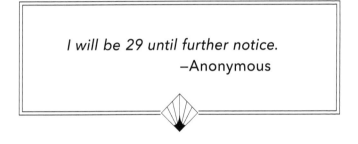

I will be 29 until further notice.
—Anonymous

THE DOWNSIZING DILEMMA

My husband and I have been empty nesters for many years now, but our nest is anything but empty. It's still overflowing with objects we know we have to get rid of but somehow never do. All those decisions! All those fond memories! All those irrational attachments! If you're like us, I'm assuming you're not a hoarder. . . are you? If you are, the American Psychiatric Association has cognitive-behavioral therapy and meds for you. But if you're just a run-of-the-mill procrastinator and hear yourself saying any of the following, know you are not alone:

I might need it some day: Doesn't the fact that you haven't "needed it" in the last ten years tell you something? Like the fact that the dress wouldn't fit even if you lost 20 pounds, and, besides, big shoulders went out with the Reagan White House. Like the fact that no one services Princess phones anymore, you can't get ribbons for that Selectric typewriter, the Walkman expired with the dodo bird, and even charities turn their noses up at your old clunker of a car.

I'm saving it for the kids: If your daughter hasn't unpacked her wedding dishes after six years, what makes you think she'll want yours? If your son eats on paper plates and uses plastic forks, why would he get excited about your heirloom Wedgewood service for 12? Get real about the silver that needs polishing, the hand-painted china that can't go in the dishwasher, and the gold-rimmed cups that blow up in the microwave. Apparently, even the Salvation Army now refuses such impractical relics of "gracious living".

I'll rent a storage unit: You're just postponing the inevitable. Americans can rationalize keeping anything and apparently we do. In 1995 just one in 17 households rented a unit; now it's one in 10. No wonder there are almost 50,000 self-storage facilities in this country, double the number of McDonald's and Starbucks locations *combined*. Moreover, on average the popular 10' X 10' storage pod costs nearly $2,000 a year. Indecisiveness costs, big-time!

But it's part of my past. Which is why it should not be part of your present. Resist wallowing because if you start reading just one old love letter, you'll be wandering down memory lane for hours. The same goes for photo albums. The solution to the latter is digitizing—which guarantees you'll never look at those photos ever again. It's unbearable to part with anything wedding-related, which is why brides schelp their wedding gown every time they move (sound familiar?). I even know a woman who kept the first slice of her wedding cake boxed up on a closet shelf for decades. Eeew!

I have just the place for it: Most of us vastly overestimate the capacity of our living space. One woman told me she was getting nowhere discarding furniture because every time she and her husband considered one of their pieces, he said breezily, "Oh, that will go into my new study." She thought to herself, "If it were the size of Versailles." She finally had to bring in a space planner to bring him down to earth.

Downsizers will tell you that when you divest yourself of possessions, you feel liberated and free to focus on what's really important, like your grown kids. But, hey, wasn't your son supposed to retrieve that 15-year-old rusty bike he's so sentimental about? And wasn't your daughter going to take back the moldy cheerleader outfit she swears represents the apex of her life? They better hurry up; curbside pickup is only three days away.

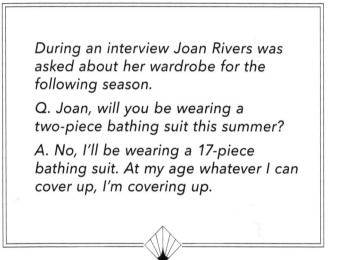

During an interview Joan Rivers was asked about her wardrobe for the following season.

Q. Joan, will you be wearing a two-piece bathing suit this summer?

A. No, I'll be wearing a 17-piece bathing suit. At my age whatever I can cover up, I'm covering up.

HEIGHT: THE LONG AND THE SHORT OF IT

When I was growing up, I was one of the tallest girls in class. I know this because in those days kids were lined up in size order, and I was always placed next to last in front of Susan Walling, she of the hearty Scandinavian stock. Except for Susan's family and a few others, ours was basically a second-generation southern and eastern European neighborhood, where people were short-ish, so I was considered tall-ish.

No more. I just had my annual physical, where I was weighed and measured. Knowing this moment of truth was coming, I pondered that trade-off peculiar to middle-aged women: should I keep my shoes on so I'll be a half inch taller or take them off so I'll be a half-pound lighter? I opted for the former, fluffed up my hair, and practiced my very best posture. Alas, to no avail. When the ordeal was over, the nurse boomed out in a voice that must have carried right through the waiting room and, from the sound of it, to all the ships at sea, that I had shrunk again, down a stunning 2" from where I had been in my prime. Aaargh! When I told my sister, she replied that we should create a ruler on the side of a door, the way we used to as kids. Only this time we'd erase from the top.

I used to love being tall. Tall connotes seriousness of purpose and leadership ability. Tall = authority. Think George Washington (6"4") and Thomas Jefferson (6'2"). Of course there was there was that shrimp Napoleon, whose press agent put out the word that he was a full 5'7", the average for his day. Oh, yeah? Then why did they name a short man's complex after him? There was also barely-there Stalin (5'6"), but as he and Napoleon don't fit my model, I'm conveniently forgetting about them. So, back to me . . . I'm sure it was due to my height that I was chosen camp color war captain although I never caught a fly ball in center field and why I was picked to star in our junior high school musical even though I couldn't carry a tune. What other explanation could there be?

Although it does not make it any easier, I realize I am not alone in my downward spiral. Studies show that almost all of us shrink as we age, and on average women lose just over 3 inches by the age of 80. Not for nothing are there phrases such as "little old lady from Pasadena." Since everything is relative, though, I have recently entertained the notion that I am not getting shorter, but rather it is the young people who are getting taller. Perhaps it is something in the milk? But if I really am to be the Incredible Shrinking Woman, I know where I can be among my own kind: The Little People of America. This organization represents anyone under

4'10", whom they consider a dwarf. The way things are going I should start preparing my membership application now.

FOXY LADY

Sexy, fashion-conscious blue-haired beauty in her 80's. I'm slim, 5'4" (used to be 5'6"). Searching for sharp-looking, sharp-dressing companion. Matching white shoes and belt a plus.

—Florida retirement complex ad

IF DROOPY EYELIDS WORKED FOR ROBERT MITCHUM, WHY DON'T THEY WORK FOR ME?

I've been battling with gravity over my eyelids for years, and gravity, alas, is winning. Ever lower my eyelids sag, and no amount of holding them up manually has stopped their downward trajectory; the outer corners just continue to lay down and die.

Oh, why can't they bring back the forties when film noir favored the sleepy-eyed look? The hardboiled gumshoe cast a sly look at the femme fatale who had just slinked into his office, and they were off to the races. The bad guys had slits where their eyeballs presumably resided when they cornered those dirty rats. And screen sirens narrowed their eyes at men with a come-hither look that made the silver screen sizzle. Robert Mitchum, the bad boy of Hollywood's Golden Age, had that look in spades. Arrested for possession of marijuana when weed was scandalous, he even did a short stint in prison. Yes, Robert Mitchum was super cool at a time when "cool" described a breeze not an attitude. And he personified the heavy-lidded look.

But then came the sixties, and impossibly large, deer-in-the-headlights eyes came into vogue. Puhleeze! No one over 30 can pull that off without looking like a pimento-stuffed olive. Yet, that's today's standard of beauty and if you don't meet it, you come across as tired, beady-eyed and—there's no way to sugarcoat it—old.

No wonder, then, that some 170,000 cosmetic eyelid surgeries are performed in the United States each year, making it the fourth most popular elective cosmetic

procedure in the country, just behind liposuc-
tion, breast augmentation and tummy tucks.
Women and, increasingly, men who can live
with liver spots, cellulite, and dowager's
hump, are undergoing "eyelid rejuvenation"
(as they call it in the biz) so they can appear
bright eyed and bushytailed. At an average
cost of $3,000 plus anesthesia, operating
room facilities, and other related expenses,
this makeover does not come cheap.

The big price tag plus the prospect of
someone coming near the vicinity of my eyes
with a knife has led me to consider some alter-
natives. The first are bangs—very long bangs.
They might tickle and probably make it hard
to see where I'm going, but, hey, no pain no
gain. The second is the veil. Veils lend an air
of mystery and ward off the sun, but perhaps
they're better suited to a nun's habit than
today's yoga apparel. A third idea is repli-
cating Joan Crawford's trick of installing pink
bulbs all over her house, thus assuring she'll

be seen in literally the most favorable light. Finally, I'm considering a course of distraction. I once read that the great beauty Babe Paley had little tinkling bells sewn into the hem of her skirts, which led me to think of installing miniscule, flashing LED lights in my headscarves. With so much going on, who would even notice that my eyelids are a bit on the droopy side?

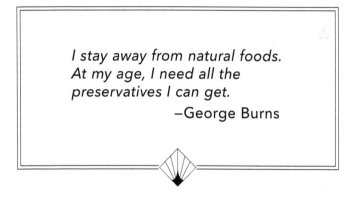

*I stay away from natural foods.
At my age, I need all the
preservatives I can get.*
                    –George Burns

HOBBIES: THE GREAT HUMBLER

When we retire we're told to try new things. I was excited to get started because I had all this pent-up crafting desire. No sooner had the adult ed catalog come out, than I was madly enrolling in every course known to woman. If they offered 'em, I took 'em: calligraphy, beginning piano, weaving, crocheting, finger knitting, quilting, book-making (not of the betting kind), basketry, and landscape design (Renaissance, drought-tolerant, and bee-friendly). I even took a course in napkin folding, although I told friends it was the history of origami. The results were less than heartening. In fact, as we used to say in New York, I stunk.

After a year of concentrated effort, I could barely play chopsticks on the piano. The rods I soldered in welding class keeled over as soon as the iron cooled. The placemats I collaged kept wrinkling and, every time I put a warm cup of coffee on them, the glue underneath melted. My bookbinding efforts yielded less than stellar results, as well. Let's just say that if I had been making the cover, we'd still be waiting for the Gutenberg Bible.

Okay, there were a few successes. I actually got reasonably proficient on the keyboard with one song, *Shortnin' Bread*, which my kids thought I should take on the road and call the *Shortnin' Bread* Tour. My ukulele efforts were rewarded with an invitation to join the Ukulele LuLus, but let's face it, they were desperate, what with being short four members and a concert coming up. My knitting class actually did result in a sweater, and I'm sure whoever took it from the "Free" table at Goodwill and entered it into the Ugliest Christmas Present Competition appreciated the effort I made.

For awhile I wanted to protest that I had attended a good college, was a respected author, and had held important jobs. But I slowly came to realize that while I might have been a hot shot in my working life, that didn't mean I couldn't be a klutz in retirement. Eventually, I came to terms with it. Yes, it is cold outside one's comfort zone, but it's exhilarating, too. I don't have to study up, improve, compete or judge my end product. My retirement anthem has become *Girls Just Wanna Have Fun*. Once I got over the need to excel, I realized that today's obsession with perfection makes anything less than that look like failure, which is sad.

Besides, I'm fighting back. This week I proudly ensconced one of my own handmade baskets between two "real" pieces in the family room and, if you stand far enough away and close one eye, you'd say it fits right in. I also sent off one of my quilts to a grandson. It's a little lopsided, but since he's only six years old, I'm not dreading his review in *Arts in America*. Actually, as soon as I get done with today's finger painting class, I'm going to ask another grandchild to wear the macaroni necklace I made. After all, I wore hers.

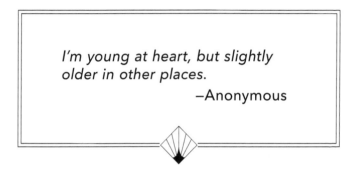

I'm young at heart, but slightly older in other places.

—Anonymous

BEAUTIFUL AT ANY AGE

Magazines have discovered the older woman. Nowadays they're running features with the title, "Beautiful at any Age," but it seems that age has to be younger than 60. After that, I guess, we're supposed to link arms and jump into the Grand Canyon lest we offend society with the sight of us. Moreover, since the purpose of magazines is to sell clothing, their young editors probably figure that after 60 we're all wearing Depends, which go with everything so we no longer have to shop.

Don't their marketing departments follow the surveys? The ones I've seen show that middle-aged woman are the only ones who are even reading magazines anymore, since the younger generation wandered into the blogosphere and never came out. Besides, without student debt, we're the ones with the disposable income.

One magazine did recently throw us a bone by putting one of our own kind on its cover and using the headline, *Fashionable at Any Age.* It's a convention that older models must have gray hair and must be super-vigorous. The stylist on this shoot really went to town with her older model, whom she clothed in an outfit more appropriate for a seraglio than a senior citizens facility. To drive home the point that we oldsters should Live! Live! Live! the model was posed on a bicycle. Did any Letters to the Editor gush over her weird harem pants and perky fez hat? (which would certainly be my go-to outfit for a quick run to Costco) No, readers were alarmed that the model was riding without a helmet, that she didn't have bicycle clips on her pants, that "who the hell wears high heels on a bike!!!" and—taking note of her long, vermillion digits—warned that nail polish can mask, and contribute to, fungus. Needless to say, it wasn't the magazine's most successful cover.

Jane Fonda, of course, is the poster child for the beautiful-at-any-age movement. I don't know about you, but I'm good and sick of magazines insisting, "This is what 80 looks like!" Good for Jane that she's still strutting her stuff as an octogenarian, but this is NOT what 80 looks like for us mere mortals and never will. The message this sends is, "Okay, maybe you have to grow old, but under no circumstances may you break America's 11th Commandment, "Thou Shalt Not *Look* Old."

Jane Fonda solved the problem of sagging skin and squinty eyes by spending zillions on plastic surgery. I have taken a cheaper but equally effective route by having my husband-the-photographer shoot me from 50 feet away or Photoshop me into anonymity. Let's face it, after a certain age, the camera is not our friend. When Gloria Swanson's silent movie queen declared in *Sunset Boulevard*, "I'm ready for my closeup now, Mr. DeMille," it proved beyond a doubt how truly delusional she had become. I wonder what today's magazines would have made of her?

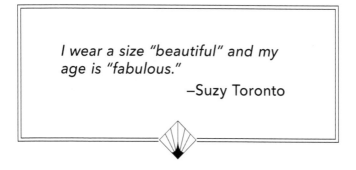

I wear a size "beautiful" and my age is "fabulous."

—Suzy Toronto

THE WORLD IS ROUND BUT MY FEET ARE FLAT

I wore a size 6 ½ shoe when I got married and I've never gotten over it. I know, I know, it's dopey to be vain about dainty feet. Nevertheless, I used to study my high arches and tell myself I had the feet of a prima ballerina. (I'm sure I couldda been a contendah if my mother hadn't given away my tutu when I was eight, for which I've finally forgiven her. I guess.) Anyway, pregnancy took care of my small feet. After carrying a child for nine months, I immediately jumped to a 7 and then, as I entered middle age, I started to wear an 8 and then an 8 ½. My brand-new sneakers are a 9, but they must run small…

How could it be that just when I'm shrinking, my feet are growing? And not just forward, they're branching out sideways, too. I trolled the Internet for the footwear equivalent of Men's Big and Tall Shops and finally found a place in Los Angeles I call the Fat Foot Store. Stylish its offerings are not but they get the job done. The "job" is getting me through the day without agony. This is no small task as most women's shoes seem to be designed by sadistic men who want to torture us so we'll stay in the kitchen—in soft slippers.

I'll concede that today's comfort shoe is somewhat more flattering than yesterday's space shoe, but, let's face it, it still doesn't have the come-hither allure of 4" platform booties, either. High heels feed men's fantasies while giving legs an elongation and elegance that Teva rafting sandals never will. Otherwise, why did Miss America contestants used to parade around in heels while wearing swimsuits, a dumb look if there ever was one?

Okay, so let's say you bow to the inevitable and decide you're going to give away all your old date night, working wardrobe, and dance party footwear. This will turn out to be a very fraught rite of passage, I can assure you. Last month I saw row upon row of old New York designer shoes in the closet of my husband's aunt, who is 96 years old. "Rosabelle," I asked, "Why haven't you gotten rid of these?" "Why should I?" she replied, "They'll come back in style one day." Never mind that she couldn't squeeze her feet into those pumps with a pair of pliers, was much too unsteady to walk in them, and would never live long enough to see their triumphant return. No, we may give away our Reed & Barton silver, Wedgewood china, and even a Steinway grand piano without so much as a backward glance, but part with a classic pair of Ferragamos? Never!

Freud once famously inquired, "What do women want?" Well, I can tell him: We want shoes to die for without the pinch that makes us wish we *had*. Is that too much to ask?

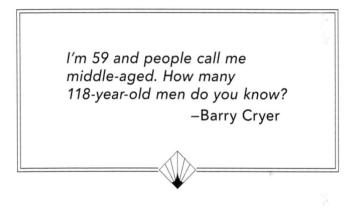

*I'm 59 and people call me
middle-aged. How many
118-year-old men do you know?*
—Barry Cryer

PURPOSE! PASSION! PEP!

It's amazing that for untold millennia people managed to age all by themselves. Today, though, we Boomers have been discovered by the self-help industry, which has wrung all it can from *Bringing Up Baby* and *Dealing with Difficult Colleagues* and has moved on to *Rescuing Retirees.* I can hardly skim a magazine, website, or blog without some blaring headline exhorting me to live out my golden years with Passion! Purpose! Pep! Apparently, we have to take classes to improve our minds, exercise daily to improve our bodies, and do good works to improve our society. With all this rushing around, retirement makes the office look good. At least there we could sit down occasionally.

I noticed, too, that all this advice assumes we're dissatisfied with our lives. Let's face it, if there's no angst, there's no article because there's so little to say to the happy. Perhaps that's why Yuppie writers are trying so hard to make us feel that we're doing it all wrong if we don't follow "The 10 Commandments of Retirement," "The 8 Best Places to Live for Seniors," or "The 15 Tips That Will Help You Live Forever."

I wonder if these young advice-givers have actually ever met anyone over 65? I ask because they seem to think of us as pathetic wallflowers who are perpetually disgruntled, sitting by the TV set for hours until we can shuffle off to our 5:30 dinner. This scenario doesn't bear the faintest resemblance to the Baby Boomers I know. In fact, we seem to be a lot more gruntled than the younger genera-tion with their opioid prescriptions, caffeine addictions, and social media distractions. More often than not when I try to book my friends, they're already engaged mentoring a high school student, attending a board meeting, planning a gala, playing bridge, swimming 20 laps, or marching for the greater good. I don't know when they sleep.

Whereas Buddha used to be the symbol of what senior citizens aspired to, now it's the Mexican jumping bean. Catching Tony Bennett at the MGM Grand was considered strenuous enough for people our age, but now we're expected to hike down the Grand Canyon, sign up for an archeological dig in the Sahara, or jump out of a plane like George Bush, Sr. if we are to be "relevant." According to the self-appointed aging gurus, if we aren't constantly in motion or feeling some vague dissatisfaction with our lives that only Getting Out There will cure, we're missing out. To all of which I say, "Whoa!"

Now, perpetual motion may be fine for some Boomers, but what of the rest of us who would prefer to stop and smell the roses? Why must we be sucked into competitive aging? Advice givers be damned, I'm all for life in the slow lane. If you are, too, say it loud and say it proud! In fact, it's a crying shame that rocking chairs have gone the way of the dodo bird because I could really do with a good rock right now. And as for that afternoon nap . . .

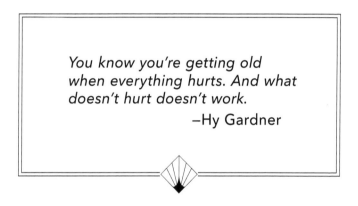

You know you're getting old when everything hurts. And what doesn't hurt doesn't work.

—Hy Gardner

WHERE, OH WHERE, HAS MY LITTLE WAIST GONE?

L ook, I'm not saying I was Long Island's answer to Scarlett O'Hara, but in my day I did have a small waist. Okay, maybe it was a bit more than a hand span, but there was a definite indentation around my middle. This is how I know: I got my wedding dress at the high-end discount store Loehmann's for $99. Even in the Middle Ages that was a very good price for an all-lace garment, so it had to have been a sample size, right? Fast forward a quarter century and my younger daughter wants to get married in that dress. She is only a size six, yet the dress has to be let out. Suddenly, the dress that originally cost me only $99 is being altered to the tune of $1,000. (It's not that I'm bitter about the cost, honestly I'm not, although I do have to say that the price gouging that goes on as soon as anyone hears the magic word "wedding" is truly reprehensible.) But I digress . . . The point is that if a dress has to be let out to be a size six, I must have had a waist back in the old days.

Alas, these are the new days. I read somewhere that the average American gains a pound a year through middle age. I gained maybe half a pound. But somewhere along the line I lost the line, and my body reconfigured itself from an hourglass to a Rorschach ink blot. It's not that I look like a linebacker, it's just that my figure has become noticeably "indistinct."

Too bad we're not living during the Renaissance, when the full-figured woman was all the rage, or even the mid-19th century, when a well-rounded lass could be an artist's muse. Today you better look like an X-ray or you're considered hopeless. For a while I bought into this, trying to whittle my waist by twisting this way and that, hoisting mega cans of Campbell's soup, and crunching my alleged core. I even tried a "foundation garment" that nips one here and lets one out there, but for some reason I found breathing an issue.

Since I wasn't having any luck changing my body, I decided to change my wardrobe:

- I gave away my belts.
- I gave away my tuck-in shirts.
- I experimented with vests (which, between you and me, cover a multitude of sins).
- I reverted to pull-up pants, so that now my wardrobe from the waist down bears a strong resemblance to that of my pre-K grandchild.

Truthfully, I don't have time to obsess over my long-lost waist because so many other parts of my body have suddenly decided to do their own thing. I mean, did aliens from Mars capture my arms and insert jiggles in them when I wasn't looking? Did some miniscule construction workers get inside my eyelids and make them droop like wilted lettuce? And who hung that "Vacancy" sign where my brain used to reside? Hmmpf! This old body, indeed!

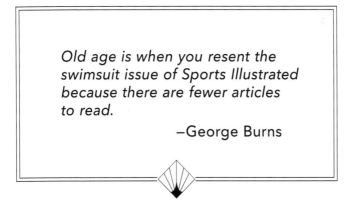

Old age is when you resent the swimsuit issue of Sports Illustrated because there are fewer articles to read.

–George Burns

PART TWO

MARRIED
SINCE THE
FIRST CRUSADE

CUDDLING BETWEEN THE COOTS

Forget the title of that famous movie about old lovers, "Love Among the Ruins." In real life getting together with someone of the opposite sex should be dubbed, "Cuddling Between the Coots." Let me say at the outset that I am a big believer in the psychic and physical benefits of cuddling. In fact, I feel a hug a day probably does a person more good than a whole bushelful of apples. The problem is how to effectuate said hug when you're of a certain age. Far removed from the days of heedless and spontaneous frisky business, we now need a strategy to get it on.

When I'm lying on the couch and my husband is sitting in his recliner, for example, canoodling requires someone to move. Right there you've got a delicate negotiation on your hands second only to the Paris Climate Accord. Were I to tootle over to sit in his lap, I might a) block his view of the Mets or b) find I could never rise again from that awkward position. We would be found entwined days later, by which time rigor mortis would have set in.

Conversely, were my husband to tear himself away from the game (very, very long odds on that one), it would be a lengthy process, a) because the Mets are only losing 24-2 in the bottom of the ninth, but you never know, they could still pull it out and what kind of fan would he be if he turned off the TV now? and b) by the time the game was over I'd be sound asleep.

Let's say for the sake of argument, though, that my husband does get up from his recliner and walk the two steps to the couch, where I have firmly taken root. How do we proceed? His left shoulder is frozen of late and my right arm goes up only so far. This makes it hard to clinch. I guess we could just sit opposite each other and pooch out our lips, but stiff necks are sure to result.

Having given up on the idea of making mad, passionate love on the couch or even patting each other on the back, we repair to bed. This is where things literally heat up. My husband is always at least 10 degrees warmer than I am, and for those of us with congenitally ice-cold digits, this is nothing to sneeze at. The problem for *me* is that he is at the other end of the California King and scooching over is not as easy as it used to be. The problem for *him* is that, warm at last, I tend to fall asleep clutching his toasty body. In fact, he says he'd need the Jaws of Life to extricate himself from my death grip. Even though I'd prefer to hear him say he'd lie awake all night and look at the ceiling in the interests of love, I see his point. So, it's back to the cuddle and where there's a will, there's a way!

MINT CONDITION

Male, 1949 model, high mileage, good condition, some hair, many new parts, including hip, knee, cornea, valves. Isn't in running condition but walks well.

—Florida retirement complex ad

MEMO TO HUSBAND:
10 REASONS WHY YOU SHOULDN'T LEAVE ME FOR A MUCH YOUNGER WOMAN

1. She'll say "like" 10 times in every sentence, driving you up the wall.

2. She'll want a baby. I can just see you getting up for the 2 am feeding, not to mention listening to the crying. Besides, babies grow up. And become teenagers. And, as you'll recall all too painfully, cost a lot of money.

3. She'll wear ripped jeans and dark glasses and walk around with a latte and/or, God forbid, a toy poodle. You hate those little yappers.

4. She'll want you to go out with her equally young friends. What will you say to them, "Why, when I was your age..."?

5. When you're dating she'll profess to love classical music and modern jazz, and then, once she has a ring on her finger, your walls with shake with the howls of rap.

6. She'll make you go on yoga retreats, eat brown rice, and slurp green, slimy shakes. Did you really think she got that tight little butt from your Big Macs and fries?

7. She'll have her eyeballs glued to her phone instead of to you.

8. You'll have to hold in your stomach, pretend to read without your glasses, and climb the steps when what you'd really rather do is take the elevator.

9. You'll have to ask her how to fix your computer glitches.

10. You'll have to do your research on Cialis, Viagra, Viril-X, Exenze, Ageless Male and Steel Libido (I kid you not) and many more. It seems there are a lot of old dudes like you trying to prove they're young.

Want to think it over?

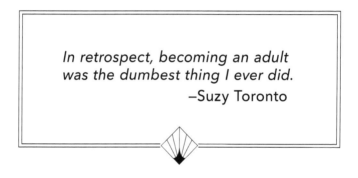

*In retrospect, becoming an adult
was the dumbest thing I ever did.*
—Suzy Toronto

A MARRIED MAN WALKS INTO A CLOTHING STORE...

There always comes a moment in the new year when I survey my retired husband's outfits. I use the term "outfits" loosely as to my eyes he could be mistaken either for a homeless person or a top Hollywood director (we live in Southern California, after all). That leads to THE DISCUSSION, and, no, it's not about whether he should be buried or cremated, but whether it's time to go clothes shopping. Believe me, this is the more fraught topic.

Me: *"Let's go through your closet first so you can see what you need."*

He, alarmed: *"I can't do that! Real men don't go through their closets. They just, um, intuit what they need."*

So Mr. Intuition and I drive to a nearby department store. We haven't even turned off the engine when he starts in:

He: *"Remind me again why we even shop here? It's so hard to find anything in their men's department."*

Me: *"Because all the other stores have gone out of business." (Their owners probably committed suicide after dealing with shoppers like you, I think but don't say.)*

We enter, he snatches a few chinos from the pile and then announces, *"Let's go."* We've been in the store six minutes, and already he's hyperventilating.

Me, reasonably: *"Why don't you try them on?"*

He: *"I don't have to, I know they'll fit. They're my size, 32 long."*

Me, silently: *Were your size back in 1987, but I hold my tongue.*

I finally persuade my husband to take a few pairs into the dressing room. They look okay except for puddling up around his ankles.

He: *"Why are they making pants so long these days?"*

Me: *"You shrank, but don't worry, we'll get them hemmed."*

He: *"At $35 a pop? No way! Rubber bands will work just fine."*

Me, moving on: *"How about some shirts to go with those pants? It's good when at least one color matches one other color on your body."*

He, holding up a gaseous green number: *"This shirt is great, it will go with everything." (I know it will go with nothing, but I feel the mother of all migraines starting to form, so I just smile and add it to our cart.)*

He: *"Do you think I need a suit?"*

Me: *"It's a good idea. I mean we're going to more funerals these days, our friends' kids are getting married, and then there are their grandchildren's communions and bar mitzvahs. . ."*

He: *"Don't be ridiculous, nobody wears a suit, anymore."*

By this time I'm wondering why I ever offered to go clothes shopping with this man. In fact, I'm wondering why I ever agreed to marry him. And that's before we get to checkout.

He: *"Look at that line!" he shouts.*

Me, icily: *"Why don't you wait in the car?"*

He: *"No, I'm going to see this transaction through!" (As if waiting behind three people at a Macy's cash register is akin to wresting the Holy Land from the Infidels.)*

Oh, why don't they just make the men's department a drive-through? It would save so many marriages, including my own.

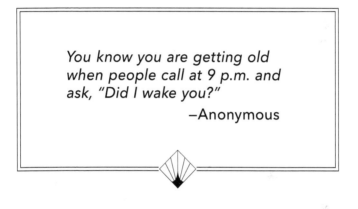

You know you are getting old when people call at 9 p.m. and ask, "Did I wake you?"

—Anonymous

A REALLY GOOD ARGUMENT

Thanks (or no thanks) to Google, my husband and I will never again have a knock-down, drag-out fight over whether Marilyn Monroe starred in "Three Coins in a Fountain" or "How to Marry a Millionaire" *(The correct answer is "How to Marry")*. We're not going to have a screaming match about who won the Kentucky Derby in 1998, Smarty Jones or Big Brown (*Neither*). And we're not going to go at it over who was born first, Jackie Kennedy or Elizabeth Taylor (*Jackie was born in 1929 and Elizabeth was born in 1932.*). Thanks a bunch, Google, for taking away that invigorating, heart-thumping slug-fest between two people who don't know what the hell they're talking about but will defend it to the death. Now, with one click or a few words whispered into Siri's ear, the case is settled once and for all. Controversy sure ain't what it used to be.

Of course, there have always been encyclopedias and other resources for finding out who is right. I was told that back in the day my mother and her sibs used to quarrel viciously over the Sunday *New York Times* crossword. When things got really explosive they called the *Times*, which at first gave the answers free, then charged a dollar, then gave up altogether because Rex Parker told all on his website.

While the *Times* was helping out on the East Coast, the Los Angeles Public Library was providing answers on the West Coast with its Southern California Answering Network. According to Susan Orlean, author of *The Library Book*, the library also came to the rescue with a late-night, call-in service called the Hoot Owl Telephonic Reference, which had a librarian standing by to answer questions long after the library closed. Its slogan was "Win Your Bet Without a Fight." Apparently, in the late evening, Angelinos liked to wager on such trivia as the correct names of the Seven Dwarfs (*Disney's version: Doc, Grumpy, Happy, Sleepy, Bashful, Sneezy, and Dopey*). Although Hoot Owl was so popular it got a call every three minutes, conservative groups decided it catered to "hippies and other night people" and got it shut down in 1976.

Those resources allowed for at least some time to argue; today we get the answers so fast on our smart phones, we don't have time to work up even a little righteous indignation at our spouse's obtuseness. In our house the burning question right now is, "Has Nancy Pelosi been 'refreshed', a.k.a. had a face lift? My husband insists not; he thinks she's just very attractive for her age. I beg to differ and I'm backed up by numerous entries on the Net, where estimates range as high as seven procedures for our esteemed Speaker of the House. "A woman her age shouldn't look that good," said Dr. Anthony Youn, a Detroit-based plastic surgeon. "She's too cosmetically surgeon-ed," sniffed another. "She should have left in a wrinkle here and there to appear more natural." I declare myself the winner of this particular dispute, but I take no satisfaction in my triumph because now the silence is deafening. Let me think… How about my saying the stew needs more salt and my husband contending it needs more red wine? Thank goodness the kitchen is still one arena where Google can't stick its nose—or it's fork.

❦

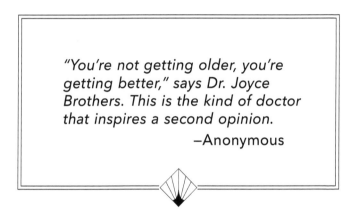

"You're not getting older, you're getting better," says Dr. Joyce Brothers. This is the kind of doctor that inspires a second opinion.

—Anonymous

MY HUSBAND-THE-ECOLOGICAL-DISASTER

When people think ecological disaster, they call to mind such large-scale catastrophes as the Great Pacific Garbage Patch, the wholesale colony collapse disorder among bees, or the 100 million trees that have succumbed to drought in California. Well, let me tell you, folks, all that is as nothing compared to the havoc my husband wreaks on the environment every day. How destructive is he—despite, as you can imagine—my many remonstrations? Let me count the ways:

- **Plastics**. When Dustin Hoffman was touted onto plastics by his future father-in-law in *The Graduate*, my husband must have been paying close attention because he never met a manmade, non-biodegradable item he didn't like. Where others swoon over leather, wool, and cotton, his mantra is "Plastics 'R Us."

- **Paper Plates**. I've spent decades trying to figure this one out, yet for the life of me I cannot understand my husband's devotion to paper plates. Does this make him feel it's not really a meal and therefore has no calories? Remind him of happy, childhood picnics? Think he'll put off emptying the dishwasher? Beats me. All I know is that faced with a choice between Royal Crown Derby bone china from England and a Vanity Fair 100-pack from Vons, he'll choose the latter any day of the week.

- **Disposable water bottles**. How irresponsible can you be? I have supplied this man with every reusable container ever devised. Some are equipped with handles, some snap onto a belt, some are metal, some have rubber sleeves, and some have nipple tops. He has a water bottle trousseau, for heaven's sakes, and yet nothing seems to beat a brand-new, squishable plastic bottle in his estimation. My only solace is that his habit allows less fortunate people to get cash for his trash at the recycling center. I'm glad someone appreciates him.

- **Styrofoam containers**. These are my husband's faves. "So lightweight yet strong, so versatile, so cheap," he coos. Does he not see the irony in organic eggs packaged in these enemies of the environment? Wake up, husband, Earth is the only home you'll ever know unless you hitch a ride on a Space X rocket, and, given your fear of heights, not to mention the $500,000 price tag, I'd say that's not a realistic option.

- **Single-serve everything.** Okay, it is really nifty to brew a cup of coffee for you and you alone, but even the inventor of the Keurig admits that the law of unintended consequences blindsided him, and now we're awash in little plastic coffee containers. But my husband doesn't stop there. From overwrapped snack packs to individual dinner entrees, he's a sucker for that pristine experience in a box.

Given his devotion to items that will last a thousand years and leach toxins into the soil throughout the millennium, I think my husband should have a landfill named after him. Let presidents, officers of the law, and local bigwigs have their names on bridges, highways, and government buildings. A much more fitting tribute to my husband would be a plaque with his likeness on it atop a plastics extruder. What a fitting tribute to an (otherwise) great guy!

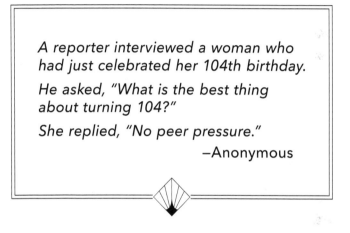

A reporter interviewed a woman who had just celebrated her 104th birthday.

He asked, "What is the best thing about turning 104?"

She replied, "No peer pressure."

                                 —Anonymous

VALENTINE'S DAY: SAY IT WITH BRISKET

My husband comes from a card-sending, gift-giving, party-for-every-occasion family. I do not. This became apparent on our very first Valentine's Day when he brought home a dozen red roses and then sat back in eager anticipation of what I had gotten him. Then he waited some more. Although this unpleasant scene played out decades ago, my husband has never forgotten it and I, thanks to him, have not forgotten it, either.

That's why I start worrying about Valentine's Day right after New Year's Eve. At least I usually do, but this year January turned out to be a hectic month and somehow Valentine's Day slipped my mind until I awoke on February 14th to find a lovely card from my husband propped up against the kitchen sink. My heart fell, but since he was still asleep, I had time to quickly write out an I.O.U. For fifty years the Florists' Telegraph Delivery Association (FTD) urged customers to "Say it with Flowers." However, in our house brisket conveys a lot more love than even the most sweet-smelling roses, so that's what I promised.

Brisket, in case you are not familiar with it, is cut from the lower chest or breast of the cow and is one of the nine primal cuts of beef. No matter how it's prepared, its essence is fatty, salty, and loaded with cholesterol—in short, it's delicious. My husband likes to think my brisket is just like the one his mother used to make. Actually, it's just like Julia Child used to make in the form of *boeuf bourguinon*, but who am I to disillusion him?

How to make this husband-pleaser, you ask? Start with a first-cut slab of meat with some fat on it, because fat conveys the flavor. Dredge the slab in flour and sauté in rendered bacon fat, butter and oil. Remove and sauté mushrooms and onions. Transfer all to a Dutch oven. I used to use hunter soup mix, but that was removed from supermarket shelves a long time ago. (Isn't that always the way? As soon as you fall in love with an ingredient, it's been made obsolete.) Anyway, add onion soup mix, beef broth to cover and—the most important ingredient of all—Madeira, and lots of it. Cook for at least three hours at 350 degrees until very tender. Then, to truly develop the flavor (unless you live in the tropics and have no air conditioning), leave the dish out overnight. My sister warns that this will cause ptomaine poisoning, but I swear I haven't lost a guest yet.

Yes, my brisket salvaged Valentine's Day this year, but it disappeared too fast to be really satisfying. Next year I may be inspired by another venerable advertising slogan, "The gift that keeps on giving." The only thing I can come up with is a dog, but what if my husband thinks I'll be the dog walker?

Bad idea. Then there's the Victorian couplet, "When this you see, think of me." He's not really the pinky ring type, but as I'm in my third day of cleaning up after the brisket extravaganza, the idea of it is very tempting.

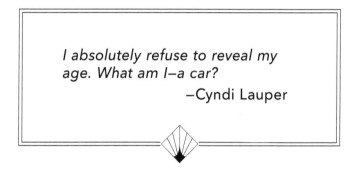

> *I absolutely refuse to reveal my age. What am I—a car?*
>
> —Cyndi Lauper

DECODING THE LANGUAGE OF LOVE

There are a lot of articles and blog posts today dealing with pillow talk, trash talk, and politically correct talk. What they don't often explore is husband/wife talk, that conversational exchange so freighted with subtext and innuendo it would take professionally trained code breakers years to figure it all out. Luckily for you, I've studied the subject and can tell you what these seemingly innocuous phrases really mean:

"I thought we agreed that..." This is the preface to any number of sentences, including but not limited to: "We're not going to your sister's for Thanksgiving ever again;" "Contributing to any charity that's not mine is O.U.T.;" and "We're no longer eating at expensive restaurants (that I don't like)."

"Tonight, I deserve to just veg out in front of the TV." Reading between the lines it spells out, "I just spent an hour and a half on the phone with Sean in Bangladesh trying to straighten out the cable bill and now I need three decades or two stiff drinks to recover."

"Jenny called." This is standard Morse code for "YOUR daughter is thinking of leaving her husband—again—and she used me as a sounding board to go over all the pros and cons. Weren't we supposed to be done with parenting when she went off to college?"

"Is that new?" This question could mean either "It makes you look fat" or "Hmm, I wonder how much that little number cost?" What it assuredly does not mean is that your spouse has suddenly become utterly fascinated by your wardrobe.

"We really need to tighten our belts." This is a not-so-subtle hint that YOU have to spend less. Go on high alert because your spouse might then let it slip he happened upon a receipt from the Shopping Channel for a 16-piece suite of ginsu knives, a purchase which you have to be ready to defend with something about withholding food if he expects you to send them back.

"The garage looks so messy." This message clearly spells out, "You need to clean up your side." The speaker has no intention of getting his hands dirty actually doing anything about the clutter, but you can tell he feels very virtuous having pointed it out.

"Let's take a trip; we really need to get away." This sentence might be music to your ears until the next note is sounded, "Are you going to plan it?" Should you demur, be prepared for, "Oh, but you're so much better at travel arrangements than I am," or, more passive-aggressively, "I would but you never like what I choose."

"You never told me that!" This is the standard default phrase when one doesn't want to go somewhere or do something. "Check your hearing aids, buddy," is what you might think but should never say. It would just lead to a lot more talking in code, and, hey, even the guy who figured out the hieroglyphs on the Rosetta Stone took a day off now and then.

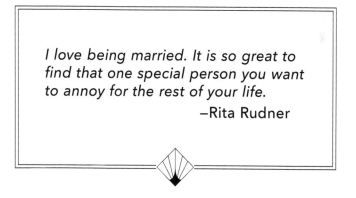

I love being married. It is so great to find that one special person you want to annoy for the rest of your life.

—Rita Rudner

BEFORE THE GPS

Before the GPS
When dinosaurs roamed the land
And hunters stalked woolly mammoths
People read maps.

That is, wives read maps
And asked the way
While husbands drove—
Around and around.

For, as my own proudly declared,
Real men don't need maps, strangers
Or wives to know where
They are going.

Before the GPS
When he had no sense of direction
(And still doesn't)
We wandered hither and yon.

In fact, one night we drove around
In so many circles looking for our new
    friends' house
I had to take a Dramamine
Before I could join the other guests.

Before the GPS
When we were lost again,
I smacked him with the map,
And said dramatically, "Stop the car,

"I'm walking home!"
Never mind that we were on a four-lane
    highway
Six states away,
And trucks were whizzing past.

Another time, lost again
And running late
I fretted that Mitzi's roast beef would be
    ruined
And he said he didn't want roast beef,
    anyway,

And I said that's beside the point
We need to be responsible guests.
And he said, how about McDonald's?
And I said, how about Reno?

Before the GPS
It's a miracle anyone stayed married.

SERENITY NOW

I am into solitude, long walks, sunrises, the ocean, yoga and meditation. If you are the silent type, let's get together, take out our hearing aids, and enjoy quiet times.

—Florida retirement complex ad

GOING WITH THE GRUDGE

I was never one to hold a grudge. In fact, that old axiom, "Never go to bed on an argument," didn't hold water for me. I thought I should *always* go to bed on an argument because by morning I'd forgotten what I fought with my husband about and therefore didn't need to make up with him.

He, on the other hand, has always been a world-class grudge holder. The Dodgers left Brooklyn in 1957 when my husband was a tot, yet he's never forgiven Walter O'Malley for pulling up stakes and heading to Los Angeles. Ever since, he's had it in for that team although they're now our home-town boys. Do you want to know why the Dodgers lost the 2017 World Series? It had nothing to do with Yu Darvish pitching two lousy games but everything to do with Jon Greenleaf putting a hex on the team sixty years ago. Believe me, you don't want to get on my husband's bad side.

Take the time he was in graduate school cramming for an exam. To hear him tell it, the only thing that got him through the night was the promise of the Milky Way he had stashed in the communal freezer. When he had stood it as long as he could, he went to retrieve said candy bar and . . . it was gone! Apparently, one of his roommates had scarfed it, and the ensuing kerfuffle made Archduke Ferdinand's assassination—which only led to WWI—look like a mere schoolyard scrap. He's still steamed up about it all these decades later.

Sophie Hannah, who wrote *How to Hold a Grudge,* would consider Jon terribly unenlightened. Ms. Hannah looks at grudges as experiences to learn from. Her 10 Tenets of the Grudge-fold Path lays out a spiffy classification system to put one on the path from dark to light. This goes hand in hand with her "grudge cabinet," in which you build narratives around the times you were wronged, grade these incidents according to their traumatizing effect, process how you felt, and then expunge your negative feelings by forgiving the transgressors.

I say, Nuts to that! While growing up I was constantly exhorted to be the bigger person, take the high road, and turn the other cheek, and by and large I got with the program. But now that I'm middle aged, I've given myself permission to be small and low, and I've found I can be as petty as the next guy. Indeed, I can see the attraction my husband has felt to grudges all these years. I've come to luxuriate in my victimhood, self-righteously railing against perceived injustices, and, especially, happily plotting my revenge. Sophie Hannah is part of the advice/gratitude/be-your-best-self industry that exhorts us to let go of anger wherever we find it. I'm sure they have a point—but only up to a point. Holding on to a little anger can be so satisfying, so cleansing, so . . . human. Would you begrudge me that?

My husband's idea of a good night out is a good night in.
—Maureen Lipman

FIVE SECRETS OF A SUCCESSFUL MARRIAGE

Herewith, wisdom from my eons of delirious marital bliss:

Secret #1: Don't Talk and Don't Listen. Never was the saying Silence is Golden more applicable than in a happy marriage. If you talk and he doesn't respond, you're ticked off. If he responds and it's not what you want to hear, you're ticked off. If you just want to vent and he's determined to solve your problem, you're ticked off. And vice versa. If there is no talk, you can both fantasize about the great conversation you just had. Besides, as we get older we all get a little hard of hearing and going silent saves us from the "What?" "What?" that can really send you around the bend.

Secret #2: A (bathroom) of one's own. As soon as our second daughter went off to college (actually, she was still in the driveway hailing her ride), I boxed up my husband's medicine cabinet stuff and carted it down the hall to the second bathroom. Heaven! I'm neat and clean, but he's over the top. He once bragged to a friend about his bathroom, *"You could eat off the floor."* The friend, to his credit, replied, *"I'd rather not."* I think I'll sneak into his bathroom one night and unscrew the cap from his toothpaste. That will mess with his mind.

Secret #3: You eat your food and I'll eat mine. Early on in our marriage I established "EMFH." That acronym stands for "Every Man for Himself," and it refers to those nights when I simply don't have it in me to rattle those pots and pans. The advantages of EMFH are manifold: a) The cook is much more appreciated on non-EMFH nights; b) I don't have to have my husband sniffing and supervising; c) I don't have to clean up his prep stuff (which for some reason is always so much more irritating than my prep stuff); and d) He gets to have the all-white meals for which he secretly yearns: eggs, potatoes, milk, and vanilla wafers.

Secret #4: Let Him Have His Fantasies–As Long As You Can Have Yours

My husband has always secretly coveted a tool belt, ten-gallon hat, and a beat-up pickup truck. Never mind that he was a suburban kid from Scarsdale who wouldn't know a lariat from a bungee cord, he's sure that one day it will be home, home on the range for him. I, on the other hand, have long entertained the perfectly reasonable dream of becoming a Ziegfield showgirl. Never mind that they were 6' tall and I'm only 5'5', that they had statuesque posture and I slump, and support hose don't go with sequins and feathers. Burlesque has been dead for years, but I can dream, can't I?

Secret #5: Practice Selective Vision. I suggest you ignore his desk with the preschool drawing on it from your granddaughter, who is now in high school. Pretend his college blazer (that will never fit him no matter how hard he holds in his stomach) doesn't exist. At the same time, do not draw attention to your wedding dress, which has hogged the front hall closet forever because you don't know where else to put it. And as for the old love letters which you both swore to throw out, there's really no need to remind him yours are stashed in the old fishing tackle box to be taken out only in case of dire depression. Speaking of old love letters, just who was that Sven who wrote me all those letters marked "Sealed with a Kiss?"

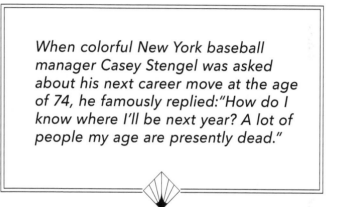

When colorful New York baseball manager Casey Stengel was asked about his next career move at the age of 74, he famously replied:"How do I know where I'll be next year? A lot of people my age are presently dead."

TO MAKE A LONG STORY SHORT

As soon as someone prefaces his remarks with "to make a long story short," I know I'm in for it. Few people are born raconteurs, yet many who go on and on—with little encouragement, I might add—think they came out of the womb slaying 'em. Professional comedians test their jokes in out-of-the-way dives to gauge audience reaction. The people who corner me at parties are oblivious to audience reaction. Nor do they seem to grasp the immutable equation that the longer the story, the less attentive the listener.

I have perfected the small, fixed smile that is suitable for every spiel from the supposedly hilarious to the graphically gruesome or heart-wrenchingly sad. This gives me cover to mentally review my supermarket list (hmm—

did that recipe call for carrots or cauliflower?), practice a few discreet stomach clenches (hey, they worked for Jane Fonda), and surreptitiously examine my nails (yes, I definitely need to throw myself on the mercy of my manicurist and get an appointment tomorrow). It also gives me time to plan the murder of my husband, who was supposed to rescue me twenty minutes ago and is still standing across the room, bending the ear of that blonde who is looking a little bored herself.

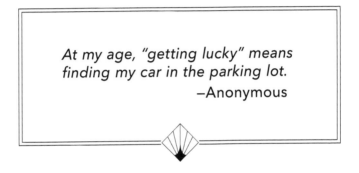

At my age, "getting lucky" means
finding my car in the parking lot.
—Anonymous

IF HE DIDN'T EAT IT WHEN HE WAS FIVE, HE AIN'T GONNA EAT IT NOW

There have always been three of us at the dinner table: I, my husband, and his kindergarten self. His eating habits are so childlike that a green has barely crossed his lips. I can't blame his limited palate on his upbringing because other people our age also had mothers from the Cheez Whiz School of Culinary Arts, and they managed to move on. Not so my beloved. His idea of the ideal day, food-wise, is scrambled eggs with fried salami for breakfast, a hot dog for lunch, and a hamburger for dinner. In the old days he would round out every meal (including breakfast) with a box of Oreos, a quart of whole milk, and a giant-size Snickers bar. He's a little more restrained now—but not much.

Of course, we all have our food hangups. I still remember my panic as a little kid when I was served liverwurst at a friend's house (I didn't return), and eggplant has never been my favorite. But I did learn to love such grown-up foods as artichokes, Brussels sprouts, and oysters. I took the try it/you'll like it approach; you-know-who didn't.

Eating out with the Food Nudge is a challenge. Suffice it to say that he's ordered *le hamburger* in such culinary meccas as Paris, San Francisco, and New York. When we finally moved to a place with no deli, I thought, "Ha! That will fix him." But no, he found three other culinary troglodytes with whom he drives once a month for one hour—more if there's traffic—to eat a pastrami on rye. They're more determined than the Four Horsemen of the Apocalypse, to whom, come to think of it, they bear a striking resemblance.

Eating in with my husband isn't much better. When I open a cookbook, I always start at "Little Kids Parties," where I know I'll find consumer acceptance. Zagat will never give my cuisine five stars, but at least my offerings don't merit an indignant, "You know I can't eat that!" True, I don't have to fuss over or even feed my husband, but it pains me that we're eating the way people did when a sandwich cost 50 cents, the TV dinner had just been invented, and a malted was considered health food. Believe me, I don't want to be married to someone who's first in line at the new Tibetan restaurant or who yearns to sample authentic Aztec cuisine. But I wouldn't mind a walk on the (mildly) wild culinary side every now and then, either.

I always felt that if you cut open my husband's veins, bologna on white would come gushing out. Now I fear that this is true of me, as well. For instead of my converting him to the delights of international cuisine, he's

converted me to the delights of school cafe-
teria fare. In fact, I think I'll rustle up a PB&J
right now. Want one? They're really good.

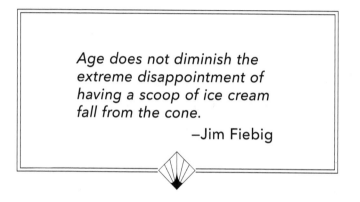

Age does not diminish the extreme disappointment of having a scoop of ice cream fall from the cone.

—Jim Fiebig

MARRIAGE: AN ACCUMULATION OF IRRITATIONS?

My husband has a cousin who summed up marriage as an "accumulation of irritations." As a newlywed I thought, *How cynical!* After fifteen years I allowed, *How depressing!* As an old married woman I think, *How true!* Here are the top ten ways my husband annoys me and I annoy him.

My gripes:

- Although I've repeatedly explained why it's more efficient to put forks down and spoons up in the dishwasher, he throws the utensils in every which way.

- He grunts when he sits down and he grunts when he gets up. "You sound like an old man," I say. "Put your fingers in your ears," he says. I roll my eyes.

- He thinks I need a supervisor—him.

- He asks what he should wear to a dinner party and, when I tell him, he insists I'm being ridiculous because nobody gets dressed up anymore.

- Speaking of parties, he's prone to accepter's remorse. "Who's coming and what is the hostess serving?" he demands. "Should I should eat first?"

- He says, "That's beside the point," when I make a point.

- He could eat off bone china, but he prefers using paper plates. This guy should be the "Don't" in the next Al Gore movie.

- He's convinced there's a club that makes his cashiers run out of tape and the drivers in front of him keep it to 35 miles per hour.

- He grew a mustache when I wasn't looking. Since he didn't ask my permission, I would never admit that it makes him look distinguished.

- His skin is better than mine although I use cream every night and he only uses soap.

His gripes:

- I'm always right. That doesn't stop him from taking very firm positions, on everything, even when he's going down in flames.

- I have a sense of direction and he doesn't. See above.

- I read faster than he does. We now share a Kindle, so we know who's at 25% and who's at 35%. There's nowhere to hide.

- I have three holes-in-one; he has two Masters degrees. (But I know he secretly wishes he had three holes-in-one, instead.)

- I slump. Now he slumps, too, but somehow my poor posture bothers him and his doesn't.

- He thinks my side of the garage is messy. He's got a point there.

- He says I leave the lights on when I leave a room. For that matter, so does he, but, oh, well.

- I can't carry a tune. "Listen!" he says. I listen and still can't carry a tune. Okay, I can sing *Darktown Strutters Ball*, which has a range from C to D, but, unfortunately, there hasn't been much call for that since 1928.

- He wants me to dump all my letters from old loves the way he did way back when. I'm not dumping.

- I'm always right.

Over the years we've gotten better at cutting each other some slack, which might be why we're still married after forty-plus

years. However, I really must take this opportunity to point out why it makes complete
sense to put spoons up and forks down in
the dishwasher...

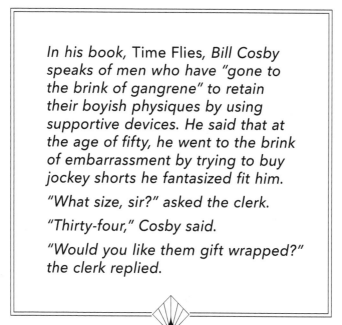

In his book, Time Flies, *Bill Cosby speaks of men who have "gone to the brink of gangrene" to retain their boyish physiques by using supportive devices. He said that at the age of fifty, he went to the brink of embarrassment by trying to buy jockey shorts he fantasized fit him.*

"What size, sir?" asked the clerk.

"Thirty-four," Cosby said.

"Would you like them gift wrapped?" the clerk replied.

WE REALLY HAVE TO ECONOMIZE!

After he finishes doling out the dough each month, my husband predictably explodes with the self-righteous declaration, "We really have to economize! I just can't keep funding these !#$%^&*()_+! credit card bills."

> **Me:** (helpfully): "I thought you wanted to build up our airline miles."

> **He:** (sarcastically): "Oh, so that's the ploy, 'You gotta spend money to make money'."

> **He:** (proudly): "Look, I only spent $12.99 on this week's groceries."

> **Me:** (skeptically) "Yes, but all you bought was a quart of milk, one roll of toilet paper, and three turnips."

He: *(resignedly)* *"There's no reasoning with you when it comes to money."*

Actually, there's no reasoning with *him* when it comes to money, so I just nod my head and smile sweetly. It's funny how the person who pays the bills starts to think of *our* money as *my* money. It's also funny how the other spouse is always the spendthrift while the payor is the model of fiscal probity.

He: *"Do you really need to go to the hair salon every week?"*

Me: *"I'm known for my impeccable grooming, and even you acknowledge that my hair is difficult. Without Dafne's sure touch I'd look like a mad scientist. How would you like that?"*

He: *"Hmmpf!"* *(But still not giving up)* *"Well, what about your manicurist? Over the years you've spent enough to send her around the world."*

Me: *"If you keep this up, I'm going with her."*

I know that even the richest people have their little money-saving tricks, such as turning the ketchup bottle upside down to wring out the very last drop or buying their Jockey shorts at Target. I once read about a celebrity who flew first class from Los Angeles to New York and then saved on cab fare by taking the train and two subways to get home. But even for regular people, saving money has become very fashionable. Like ripped jeans, it's a kind of reverse snobbery. Whereas the upwardly mobile used to tear out clothing labels from déclassé shops, they now brag for all to hear, "I got it at Ross Dress for Less!" Soon, like Minnie Pearl, they'll be hanging the discount price tag from the front of their hats.

All of which brings us back to my husband, a.k.a. Ebenezer Scrooge. Don't you dare tell him, but I've decided to swim against the tide, prop up the economy single-handedly, and pointedly ignore the cost of everything. I want to be bigger than that money-obsessed person who knows the cost of everything and the value of nothing. So, you see, it's really to propel me along my spiritual journey that I'm now sailing past the sales rack, ordering à la carte and throwing away my mail-in coupons. I mean, at this age, aren't we actually living on our children's inheritance? And one thing's for sure, they'll know how to spend it.

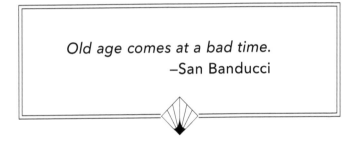

Old age comes at a bad time.
—San Banducci

THE PRINCE OF DARKNESS

When I refer to the "Prince of Darkness," let's be perfectly clear (even in this dim light) that I'm not talking about Beelzebub or even Lord Voldemort. I'm describing an otherwise normal husband who happens to have a thing about keeping his wife in the dark—literally. According to one energy calculator, running a 60-watt bulb for 8 hours costs 12 cents. So why, when a gallon of gas costs $3.36, a hot dog costs $4.29, and a room at Motel Six costs $84, is my husband obsessing over a measly 12 cents? It's one of those inexplicable mysteries of nature, like why is the sky blue and why is the ocean gray? After all these years, the best answer I can come up with is, *because*.

I don't think my husband realizes that the light bulb is not a new idea. Lauded in various scientific histories as "one of the everyday conveniences that most affects our lives," the bulb was originally conceived by Humphrey Davy in 1806, when he demonstrated a crude device called the arc lamp. Then along came Thomas Alva Edison 73 years later with the first commercial incandescent light. Still, progress was slow. Most Americans continued to light their homes with gas and candles for another fifty years, and, as late as 1925 only half of all American homes had electric power. You know which half my husband would have been in.

But suffice it to say, he doesn't stop at light. For him the words "cold" and "dark" go together like "peanut butter" and "jelly." As far as my husband is concerned, money spent on heating is money thrown out the window. Of course, he never gets cold so he can't understand why, when other women are stripping down to their PJ's or skimpy nighties to go to sleep, I'm donning enough layers to keep a climber warm on Mt. Everest. As luck would have it, every so often my ice-cold feet might migrate over to his side of the bed, reminding him that one of us is not happy with the sub-zero temps in our house. But that's always accidental, right?

The idea of banishing cold by way of central heating is far older even than the electric light bulb. Although sources differ as to whether the Romans started warming their temples, baths, and homes this way in 350 BC or 80 BC, you get the picture that central heating wasn't born yesterday. Called hypocausts, the Romans' ingenious system distributed heat from an underground fire through a space beneath the floor, thus warming both floors and walls. It is considered one of the Roman Empire's greatest achievements, a pronouncement I heartily second.

Unfortunately, my husband must have skipped school the day that lesson was taught, which is why, should you ring my doorbell, you'll find me wearing a miner's light and carrying a portable heat lamp. These accessories may not earn me a spot on the best-dressed list, but while I'm married to the Prince of Darkness, they beat a Gucci outfit any day.

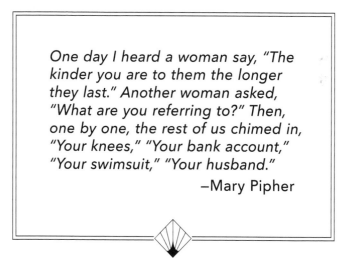

One day I heard a woman say, "The kinder you are to them the longer they last." Another woman asked, "What are you referring to?" Then, one by one, the rest of us chimed in, "Your knees," "Your bank account," "Your swimsuit," "Your husband."

—Mary Pipher

PART THREE

MUDDLING THROUGH MODERN LIFE

AND HOW ARE YOU?

As far as I'm concerned, the only acceptable response to the polite question, "How are you?" is the equally polite response, "Fine." Sadly, though, a whole generation didn't get the memo and that generation is now mine. Once upon a time it was only my Uncle Willie who, when asked "How are you?" actually went into detail, but now a shocking number of my contemporaries have taken up the tell-all cudgel. Why? They're not running for president, so why do we need to know?

Maybe Lyndon Johnson had to bare his gall bladder scar and Dwight Eisenhower had to circulate his cardiogram to reassure the populace that they would live out their terms, but Morty Dunkelmeyer, the Buick dealer who lives two doors down? I don't think the American people will rest any easier in their beds knowing that, although his blood pressure registered 150 over 100 at his last reading, he's now taking Lopressor to lower it. And as for his trick knee . . .

No, I do not need to know what the X-ray of Morty's hip revealed, why he needed an MRI, and how he really should go for another CAT scan but it will have to wait until after his colonoscopy. And though his overall cholesterol reading is over 200, his HDL, the "good" cholesterol, is so much higher than his LDL, the "bad" cholesterol, that his doctor is holding off on the Lipitor for now. As my eyes glaze over and my mind desperately reaches out to my happy place, I ruefully reflect that, with the Mortys of the world, you get the diagnosis and the prognosis but, alas, never the synopsis.

After a certain age, too, every communal get-together seems to start with a 15-minute organ recital, and it's not of the hymnal sort. Based on these orations I would say that America is now not only the arsenal of democracy, it's also the arsenal of home remedies. Our bathrooms are chock full of muscle relaxants, Ace bandages, Epsom salts, heating blankets, knee braces, arm slings, and wrist supports. And those are only the orthopedic fixes.

Even though I'm definitely not discussing health, I secretly hope you have a feel-better tip for me. If you don't, then you're the only one. Everyone else I know is loaded with advice, and they're adamant about it. Have a delicate stomach? You must try the Low Fodmap (Paleo, Mediterranean, Atkins) diet. Got a bad back? You have to use my chiropractor (yoga instructor, acupuncturist, tai chi practitioner). Actually, if you're really uncomfortable, nothing beats two acetaminophens and two ibuprofens. But, as I have taken a vow of silence when it comes to medical issues, you didn't hear that from me.

MEMORIES

I can usually remember Monday through Thursday. If you can remember Friday, Saturday, and Sunday, let's put our two heads together.

—Florida retirement complex ad

10 INGENIOUS SOLUTIONS TO PROBLEMS I DIDN'T KNOW I HAD

Once upon a time Americans didn't know that having breath that smelled like the inside of an old sneaker was a bad thing. Then someone invented halitosis and we've been swigging Listerine ever since. Other manufacturers soon caught on, and the mania for creating problems that demand paid solutions has been with us ever since. I particularly like these catalogue entries:

1. **Orthodontia for your toes.** I never knew crooked toes were such a scourge that sufferers would wear separator socks, mini-splints, and tiny Ace bandages to keep them straight. It seems to me it

would be easier to trade in your flip-flops than strap on all that paraphernalia, but who am I to judge?

2. **Concierge care for your baseball caps.** There are over-the-door hangers for your trousseau of headgear, forms to reshape them after washing, and stuffing to help them stay in tip-top form. But, dare I ask, when are you going to wear 54 baseball caps, anyway?

3. **Beer cap map of the United States.** Here's a way to show off your prized collection because there's a hole in each state for one of your finest bottle caps. Thoughtfully accompanied by a jute cord, the map can easily be hung up, replacing that tacky old original Picasso currently hanging over your fireplace.

4. **Cap visor lights.** These are little LED strips that you can clip onto any cap, where they will emit a steady beam or

flashing signal. I can only imagine the screams coming from the user's wife when he re-enters the bedroom after clapping on the hat to find the toilet at 2 a.m. Miner's pick optional.

5. **Small animal booster car seat.** This plush seat allows smaller pets to look out the window. I don't know if Fido has any interest in the outside world (he never said), but doting pet owners will feel better knowing they've given a cherished family member the opportunity to literally expand his horizons.

6. **Toilet bowl gleamer.** "The middle-of-the-night bathroom solution is here!" Thanks to LED lights, the bowl glows green when the seat is down and red when it is up. The catalog claims it's a great solution for the whole family. "Brilliant!" I believe is their word. Bring your own AA batteries and a sense of humor.

7. **Sled Legs.** These wearable mini-snowboards, when attached to the lower half of your legs, allow you to slide downhill on your knees, which, admit it, is something you've always yearned to do. The big advantage, they claim, is that there's no heavy sled to drag back up. Look for Sled Legs on clearance.

8. **"How to Swear Around the World."** Since this is billed as the perfect family coffee table book, one can only wonder to what family they are referring, Don Corleone's? It is thoughtfully illustrated "to assist you in your worldwide swearing abilities." Adults say the darndest things...

9. **Potato Chip Grabber.** As the catalog boasts, "Every once in a while an invention comes along that is so revolutionary that it changes the world forever . . ." This gizmo allows you to eat messy snacks without getting your hands all sticky

and gross. Actually, I have an even better idea—give up junk food.

10. **Mega Door Hanger.** This uber-functional storage unit holds up to 30 pairs of shoes, eight small purses, and probably six gerbils. Never mind that you don't own 30 pairs of shoes and the sheer weight of the piece will cause your door to fall off its hinges and die. I mean, nothing in this world is perfect, especially when it only costs $19.99.

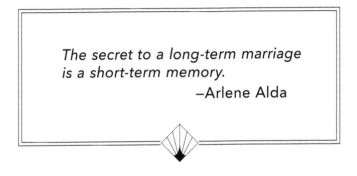

> *The secret to a long-term marriage
> is a short-term memory.*
> —Arlene Alda

BABY BOOM

I like children. If they're
properly cooked.
                     and
Get out of here, kid; you
bother me.
                     —W.C. Fields

B abies are now those without whom no
photo shoot is complete, but it wasn't
always that way. Once upon a time a long time
ago in the Kingdom of Hollywood, nobody
had babies, at least not publicly. Studios
invested a lot of time and money in creating
glamour puss images for their female stars
and maternity garb definitely did not fit that
image. No dummies they, the actresses held
in their stomachs or wore girdles as long
as they could and then, when they couldn't
hide being *enceinte* anymore, they simply
dropped out of sight for a few months, only

to re-emerge with their girlish figures intact. Nobody said boo about a baby.

When a star's family included older children, a tasteful spread at Christmas would feature everyone perfectly neat, clean, and preppie. Other than that, children in Hollywood were neither to be seen nor heard. Not anymore. And, I ask you, where is W.C. Fields when we need him? Don't get me wrong, I like kids, I have kids, I even have grandkids. But honestly, our society's obsession with celebrity-as-Madonna (the Biblical not the *Material Girl* kind) is simply getting icky sticky.

The gushing starts with the notorious baby bump. In case we should miss it, celebrity mothers-to-be are always photographed with a hand cradling their stomach as if their babies would tumble to the ground if they didn't hold them up manually 24/7. Future fathers likewise have their hands glued to the bump with the obligatory toothy grin telegraphing, "Aren't I the greatest to make this kid!" It's hard to get away from baby mania even if you don't read the fan-zines. Take my husband–who wouldn't know Kim Kardashian from Ara Parseghian–even he was aware that Kate Middleton was having morning sickness with her third child. And how many millions of us waited breathlessly for Meghan Markle to "show"?

As someone who reads *People* and *Us*–but only as sociological research, I assure you–I can't help but notice the rapturous delight we seem to take in celebrities-as-parents. "Ooh," the magazines gush under a photo of Sandra Bullock with cotton candy smeared all over her face and her kid's. "They eat junk food just like us!" Or, Nicole Kidman and company at the beach. "They play in the sand just like us!" My personal favorite is the shot of some well-known actress running through an airport clutching a child to her breast as if she were being pursued by a pack of wild boars. Carefully out of camera range, of course, is the phalanx of nannies and handlers who will take over with the kid as soon as the paparazzi are gone. And didn't said actress ever hear of a stroller?

Yes, social media and print magazines are infantilizing America in more ways than one. But I, for one, am having trouble buying into the hype surrounding celebrity motherhood. Let's face it, either you are chaperoning Miss Griggs's second grade class to the Statue of Liberty or you're doing a photo shoot for *Vogue*. You simply can't be in two places at once. Unless you're in the movies.

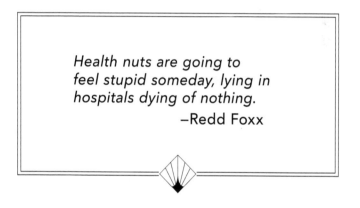

Health nuts are going to feel stupid someday, lying in hospitals dying of nothing.
                        —Redd Foxx

KALE IS THE HOLY GRAIL—THIS WEEK

Depending on the week or year
The key to good health is finally here
Biblical grains were in for a while
But amaranth failed to make people smile.

A plant-based diet is now all the rage
Filling magazines page after page
Chocolate was bad until it was good
Now French fries aren't even a food.

Who knew?

Nutritional info on Snickers?–Get real!
White meats are good, pork and veal
My doctor says okay to a little
Alas, today's vittle is not just a vittle.

My head is spinning from all the advice
Brown, organic or plain white rice?
Beef is fine for protein needs
But only grass-fed from the very best
 breeds.

Oh, why doesn't bacon grow on a tree?
Why aren't cookies good for me?
Apple, orange, pear, and peach
Recommended dose: a half cup each.

If I do it all right, I'll be 101
But who wants that if eating's no fun?
Instead, I'll chuck food as medicine
And gleefully wallow in dietary sin.

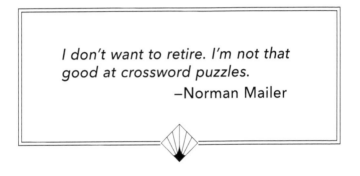

I don't want to retire. I'm not that good at crossword puzzles.
—Norman Mailer

OVER THE RIVER AND THROUGH THE WOODS

Over the river and through the woods,
To grandmother's house we go.
The horse knows the way to carry the
   sleigh
In the white and drifted snow, oh!

Remember singing that Thanksgiving song in elementary school? Well, even if global warming hadn't taken care of the snow, the sleigh would have broken down long before reaching this grandmother's house due to the sheer weight of all the paraphernalia my children and grandchildren feel is necessary for a three-day family reunion.

Let's start with the new parents. They have done the math and come out with this equation: 9 pounds of baby = 964 pounds of gear. There's the baby monitor, fold-up pram, car seat, sling, port-a-crib, mobile for said crib, special sleep sounds recorder, 33 changes of costume, lotions, and potions, not to mention the baby's special organic food and the gadgets needed to grind it down. The concerned parents round out this agglomeration with a humidifier for dry nights, a de-humidifier for muggy nights, and a HEPA filter for bad air.

Then there's our 13-year-old grandson, who assures me he's only bringing the bare necessities of life, which in his opinion are: his X-Box, a dozen color-coded cables, and a backpack that converts to a camp chair (from which one presumably can catch a trout, shoot a duck or launch a missile attack. None of these is too likely in Santa Barbara, but I guess it's good to be prepared). His equipment is augmented by a 23" TV monitor, routers, and earphones so gigantic they could be used to guide a 747 to its docking space.

His 15-year-old sister is not far behind. What is it with kids taking their pillows with them wherever they go? And I'm not talking about small, blow-up numbers, either, but the big, honking kind I've seen teens carry onto trains, planes, buses and even a Broadway show. My granddaughter has a roll-aboard suitcase and, like her brother, a 100-pound backpack. What makes it so heavy, do you think? Perhaps it's her six pairs of hip, ripped jeans. They are absolutely identical, but when I ask her why so many, she replies, "I need options."

Their mother has her own idiosyncratic baggage: a trousseau of portable chargers so versatile that were you cast into the sea, your cell phone would still be working— and flashing a light to signal rescuers. Not counting on a shipwreck anytime soon? Then perhaps you can relate to her special weighted blanket, with its BPA-free, non-toxic, hypo-allergenic polypropylene pellets.

Never mind that I've provided enough quilts to line a chieftain's yurt, my daughter assures me that only her own magic weighted blanket will lull her to sleep.

For his part, my son-in-law either became a survivalist when I wasn't looking or deluded himself into thinking he was climbing the Matterhorn instead of just driving up the 101. Otherwise, why would he have bought out the entire dried fruit and nuts section of Whole Foods? Santa Barbara is not exactly the Outback; in fact, we've got a supermarket on almost every corner. But who am I to suggest he could provision himself very well here? I'll keep mum and just feed the birds with the leftovers.

It will be my turn to visit all of them next, but I swear I'm only bringing a small carry on. Okay, maybe a small carry on plus a few items I simply can't live without for three days. But that's it. Until I start packing.

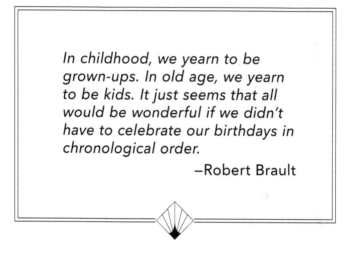

In childhood, we yearn to be grown-ups. In old age, we yearn to be kids. It just seems that all would be wonderful if we didn't have to celebrate our birthdays in chronological order.

—Robert Brault

IS THERE A QUESTION IN THERE SOMEPLACE?

To me Q. and A. after a speech should consist of audience members going to the microphone, inquiring about something the speaker said, and, one sentence that ends in a question mark later, take their seat. Today, instead of asking a question, many people deliver an op-ed. They tell us who they are, why the speaker should pay close attention to what they have to say (I never understood why being a dentist for 23 years qualified one as an expert in foreign policy, but there you go . . .), and what needs to be done to rectify a) the credit crunch; b) the sorry state of education; and c) the mystery meat they pass off as a Grade A hamburger at Susie's Korner Kafé.

By the time the alleged inquirer is winding down, everyone, including the speaker, has started to nod off. I would say especially the speaker. His eyelids have lowered, his mouth has gone slack, and his whole body is listing dangerously toward the water pitcher. I personally think he's entitled to take a little nap because the audience has just cut a whole bunch of zzz's themselves thanks to his 45-minute peroration on—something or other. In fact, many of them, including me, wish he'd come back soon as they haven't slept this well in years.

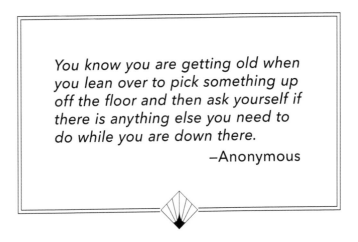

You know you are getting old when you lean over to pick something up off the floor and then ask yourself if there is anything else you need to do while you are down there.

—Anonymous

ROCK CONCERT REDUX

My husband and I attended a rock concert for "people of a certain age" the other day. It was a matinée, of course, as we and our peers tend to conk out now at evening performances.

The concert organizers certainly knew their audience because they handed out complimentary earplugs with the program. It's a wonder they didn't provide backrests and reading glasses, too. Fortunately, I had thought ahead and brought my own. Unlike concerts of old that were not for the old, no sweet smell of marijuana permeated the air. I could see that the only Mary Jane this crowd would be consuming was prescription CBD for their aches and pains.

After we took our seats, turned off our cell phones, and inserted said earplugs just in case, the trip down memory lane began. More than 40 years after first hearing these songs of the late sixties and seventies, I recognized every tune and remembered every word, which I proceeded to sing, much to the chagrin of the man on my right, who indignantly turned off his hearing aid. What a grump! Anyway, I never fail to marvel at the staying power of pop music. I might have forgotten all the subjects I studied in high school, but give me the intro to *Blowin' in the Wind* and I have perfect recall.

As you might imagine, this oldies concert focused a lot on Woodstock with blowups of half-naked, face-painted, bandana-wearing hippies looming large on the stage's big screens. I don't know about your kids, but mine just assume that all of us who lived through those times were daisy-carrying, peace-sign flashing, tie dye-wearing drop-outs. I hate to disillusion the younger generation, but this girl was a notebook-toting, circle-pin-sporting, pink and green Ivy League wannabe in Pucci knock-off shifts. The only hand-dyed fabric I knew was madras and that was strictly for Bermuda shorts. Nor would I have been caught dead at Woodstock. I mean you had to sit on the ground and use porta-potties there. Feh! If the truth be told, I was never really in touch with my inner child even when I *was* a child. Let's just say I was extremely well acquainted with my inner middle-aged accountant.

So, while I vibed to the songs of protest and passion of that era, I have to confess that I myself was manning no picket lines nor organizing any marches. (I don't count the time we housewives boycotted our local A & P because it stocked tomato soup and goldfish crackers and little else.) Still, I was a woman of my time, so at the oldies concert I felt entitled to get nostalgic over *Marrakesh Express* and *Lovin' Feeling* the second time around.

I mean, what else have I got today musically? To me it isn't music if there's no melody, which means rap is out. Besides I'd need subtitles and a 12-year-old to tell me what I was hearing. At this stage of the game, Captain Cardiac and the Coronaries are more my speed. I understand they're coming up this way, so please save me a seat—but only for the matinée.

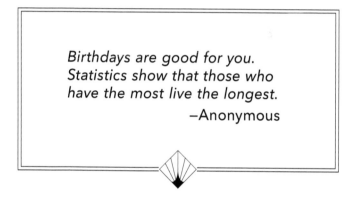

*Birthdays are good for you.
Statistics show that those who
have the most live the longest.*

—Anonymous

THANKSGIVING:
THE HOLIDAY MEAL FROM HELL

In depictions of Thanksgiving dinner circa 1952, when Mother came out of the kitchen she was perfectly coiffed and dressed to the nines in high heels, stockings, and a ruffled hostess apron. She was inevitably beaming as she presented her equally well-scrubbed family with the ultimate token of her love: a plump, glazed turkey. We could rightfully assume that everyone dug into said bird in unison: one dish, one ensemble of happy diners. Oh, thems were the days! Last Thanksgiving I had so many custom orders that, unlike that Donna Reed look-alike of the 1950's, I emerged from the kitchen with jumpy eyes, disheveled hair, and a nervous tic. Here's why:

- George had suffered a mild heart attack and couldn't eat fat.

- Cyndi had seen a movie on the industrialization of food production and no longer ate anything with eyes.

- Mike had tested high for blood sugar, so no dessert for him.

- Lucy was all in on the Paleo diet and just wanted to gnaw on some bones.

- Alice insisted on an Old Testament mix based on spelt called Scripture Bread. "It embodies thousands of years of unbroken human-plant co-evolution, effort and reverence," she intoned to the multitude. "Gag me with a spoon," I intoned to myself.

- Susie had a gluten intolerance and not only wouldn't eat the stuffing, even the salad dressing was out. (It's amazing all the products that contain gluten. Who knew?)

- Little Benny never took to vegetables, so it didn't occur to me to serve him greens. Even I had to admit, though, that an all-white plate isn't the healthiest for a kid, but, I rationalized, it was only for one night and then it was his parents' problem.

- Peter is okay with almonds, peanuts, and cashews but is highly allergic to walnuts. OMG ... which nut did I put in the apple pie topping and how many pieces did he eat?

- The baby, I was told in no uncertain terms, only eats organic.

- Pam is a passionate environmentalist, who says animals give off more carbon dioxide than cars (junk science , as we now know, but it's an article of faith with her) so she is not about to perpetuate the destruction of the planet by eating anything that walks.

- Sujin exhibited the Asian preference for dark meat, which she said is tastier than white, but since she eats almost nothing anyway, I registered her opinion and then promptly disregarded it.

- Marissa recently lost 43 pounds and was watching her calories—need I say more?

- Ginny wanted tofu turkey, which is the most disgusting thing I ever saw.

- Marcy threw around the term "plant-based" so often that I wanted to throw her around. Give it a rest, already, I thought; we get the picture.

- Derek, a devotee of the Food Channel, swore the only way to make roast turkey is to soak it in brine and insert herbs under its skin. There was more about oven temperature, resting temperature, roux, and tin foil, but, honestly, by that time I'd hit the sherry and couldn't give a flying fig.

In fact, with all these designer Thanksgiving requests, I had completely lost my appetite. Next year I think I'll serve bread and water—but I'll hold the bread, especially if it's made with spelt and was featured in the Old Testament.

BEATLES OR STONES?

I still like to rock, still like to cruise in my Camaro on Saturday nights and still like to play the guitar. If you were a groovy chick or are now a groovy hen, let's get together and listen to my eight-track tapes.

—Florida retirement complex ad

CLOTHES MAKE THE (WO)MAN—OR NOT

She dons lots of turquoise and silver jewelry
To show that she is one with her fringe-
Bedecked sisters as they stomp out
The rain dance to the beat of
    throbbing drums.

Never mind that no buffalo roamed
    anywhere near
Her ancestral home, which was actually
    a fifties
Split-level in the suburbs of Cleveland,
Close to the local Burger King.

She prefers big, clear glasses and
    no makeup
Lest people miss the point that she
    is a Thinker,

A Serious Person who ponders how
    Earth was formed
And what is the meaning of Life.

Even though in her heart of hearts what she
    really enjoys
Are reruns of "Friends," books with lots of
    pictures, and
The wit and wisdom of Cheech and Chong.
    Still,
She knows how to dress to impress.

Which means buying jeans
With a rip to show she is hip or rumpling
    her clothes
To confirm her obsession with matters
    too lofty
To even discuss with mere mortals.

Despite the fact that she's an accountant by
Day and a ferocious bowler by night,
Or that she likes tuna-noodle casseroles and
(Dare we say it it?) clog dancing.

Because in addition to being a Thinker,
She's also an Artist
Who lives to Create. It is
Who she is, it is what she Does.

Although, truth be told, it would help
If she could draw more than a stick figure
And her idea of Real Art wasn't some
Sad-eyed kid painted on black velvet.

Eventually, won't she have to admit,
That while she may be what she eats,
She is not now and never will be
What she wears?

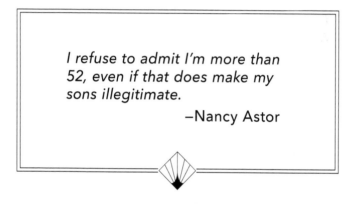

I refuse to admit I'm more than 52, even if that does make my sons illegitimate.

–Nancy Astor

SUE ME, I'M JUST NOT A CAR GUY

I admit that I'm mechanically challenged, but I think you'll have to agree that cars have become very complicated. Since the driver's manual is three inches thick and written in Urdu, it hasn't been much help in getting me to understand the ins and outs of my vehicle. As a result I never learned:

- **How to change the clock.** It is always Pacific Standard Time in my car no matter what the season. Moreover, the car clock loses a minute every so often, so I have to keep checking my watch (which isn't all that reliable, either) to make sure I'm neither too early nor too late. In my defense, this is a six-step maneuver that has even flummoxed my husband-the-techie.

188

Besides, isn't there's an overemphasis on time in our society?

- **How to program the radio.** As a result of my ineptitude, it's all-NPR-all-the-time in my car. Usually, the station is interesting and informative, but it also carries those interminable reports from Syria that make you want to slit your wrists. I do have two other options, although they are both in Spanish. I can move the dial to the religious station, where I am assured repeatedly that all is forgiven, or I can move it to the sports station, where I get the play-by-play from soccer matches around the world. Now you see why it's back to NPR.

- **How to fill the gas tank.** It isn't that I haven't tried (half-heartedly), but this particular maneuver eludes me. Afraid of my running out of gas in the Kalahari Desert, my family once made it their mission to teach me. The daughter who trains animals was patient, the one who's peppery got more so (Do you think it's because I pulled out the nozzle too soon and sprayed her all over with gasoline?), and my husband got to embrace his inner martyr. Now, I just roll into the local car wash and say to the attendant, "Fill 'er up!"

- **How to find the window washer.** Luckily we've been in a drought for five years, so this hasn't been a biggie, but every so often a bird dive bombs my windshield and I want to get off the glop. (Good old Windex and a rag to the rescue.) The windshield wipers are also an issue. Even if I can get them to start, I can't seem to get them to stop. When it hasn't rained in years and your wipers are still swiping, you get funny looks on the road, let me tell you.

- **How to i.d. my car if it were stolen.**
I worry about this because the make and model are not exactly on the tip of my tongue, and in eight years I haven't memorized my license plate, either. The registration would have that info but it's in the car so if it is stolen that doesn't do me much good. Oh, well, my car has been way too beaten up by crazed shoppers in the Trader Joe's lot for anyone to want it. Now, when I get a new car…this time I swear I'm going to read the manual.

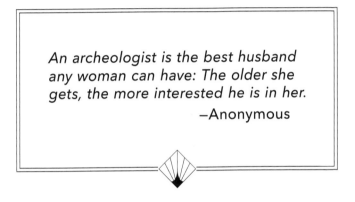

An archeologist is the best husband any woman can have: The older she gets, the more interested he is in her.

—Anonymous

WHAT IS IT THAT YOU DO, EXACTLY?

When I first became engaged, I proudly told my father, a bricks and mortar kind of guy, that my fiancé was an advertising account executive. He looked at me quizzically, then asked "Is that a real job?" Ha! If my father had trouble wrapping his arms around "advertising account executive," he should try getting a handle on what our grown children are doing today.

The traditional, hierarchical titles, such as vice president, director, manager, etc. are on their way out and playful titles are on their way in. These new, creative, titles supposedly energize team members and are an effective recruiting tool—except when job seekers can't figure out what the heck the company is talking about, which is not infrequent. Here's a Help Wanted listing that makes the point:

Brand Activation Manager, Millennial Connector Brands Department. *This person is responsible for collaborating with field sales in the translations and localization of the National Brand Priority Calendar. Based on the market designation/dynamics, he/she will be responsible for leading collaboration with the chains team in interpreting, developing, and executing the national brand plans at the customer level…in that channel.*

The top five of today's fanciful job descriptions are "rockstar," "genius," "guru," "wizard," and "ninja." And this is not just in California or in high tech. From Oregon to Maine, recruiters are jazzing up their job titles to make mundane work sound glamorous, such as Time Ninjas (a.k.a. Human Resources, which once upon a time was Personnel) and

Duct Changing Guru (which is better known as Handyman). And don't forget to greet the Director of First Impressions who started life as the Receptionist.

Title inflation, like grade inflation, is spreading. Some real examples from real companies—I mean you couldn't make this stuff up—include the recruiter who is now a Talent Acquisition Specialist, the flack who is called a Brand Evangelist, and the fund-raiser who's been reborn as a Growth Hacker. I get a particularly big kick out of that mysterious individual, the Customer Happiness Specialist. Who is this person? He/she may be an out-of-work actor sitting on a hard plastic chair in a basement boiler room trying to calm down irate subscribers whose Internet, TV, and phone have all crashed at the same time. Or he/she may be a Harvard MBA trying to persuade eBay that it better install a new, billion-dollar software system or Amazon will eat its lunch.

Few companies may have a Security Princess on the roster like Google or a Galactic Viceroy of Research Excellence as Microsoft once did, but many have the Ambassador of Buzz and the Project Meanie. Finally, at the top of the food chain you have such titles as Chief Cheerleader, Chief Amazement Officer, and Chief Troublemaker. It seems that while these CEOs are espousing highly democratic organizations, for some reason they are loathe to give up their identity as "Chief."

If it's any consolation, when it comes to your adult children's vocation, it's not you, it's the world in which they live. Eventually, you'll get it, sort of, and in the meantime you can always read Jane Austen. *Her* you can understand. As for me, I knew the jig was up when I saw my first ad for a writer headlined, "Wanted: Content Provider." *Sic transit gloria.*

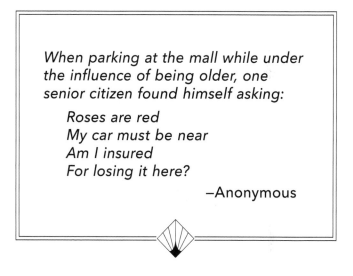

When parking at the mall while under the influence of being older, one senior citizen found himself asking:

Roses are red
My car must be near
Am I insured
For losing it here?

—Anonymous

YOU SHOULDDA BEEN HERE LAST WEEK
THE FISHERPERSON'S LAMENT

I always set out with the greatest of hopes
That on this day I will score
The Moby Dick of rainbow trout
Or at least get enough action
That warranted putting on my waders.

But as the hours pass without a bite
My eyes bleary from looking at ripples
That turned out to be—ripples
And my backside sore from the hard
    wooden bench,
The guide starts to thrum his familiar trope:

"You shouldda been here last week
Before they released the cold (or hot)
Water from the dam

And the river wasn't so high (or low)
Oh, it was just perfect last week.

"When there was enough cloud cover
And a light rain fell (or a pearly sun shone)
And we could have fished the real good
    fork
Because my shuttle driver hadn't left town
(Or gotten a flat).

"Why, last week the fish jumped themselves
    into the net
And I hadn't run out of Woolly Buggers
    (or nymphs)
Which is what you actually need on this
    stretch
Especially when the wind isn't whipping
    (or too calm)
Like today."

I feel I've heard this tune before
And I would even sing along if I weren't so
    bummed

For I, too, have a lament and it goes
    like this:
"Why can't last week be this week,
Just this once?"

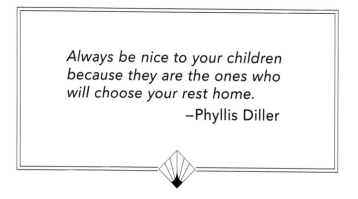

Always be nice to your children because they are the ones who will choose your rest home.

–Phyllis Diller

I GOT THE MIDDLE SEAT BLUES

On airplanes I seem to be invariably wedged between the winner and runner-up of the World's Most Annoying People contest. Maybe the airlines are getting their revenge because I tend to book late and bring great food that makes their cardboard snacks look like, well, cardboard. Whatever the reason, it seems to be my fate to share the friendly skies with those who drive me up a wall.

Who's flying today, you ask? On my right I've got the long-haired beauty, who keeps gathering her locks into buns that immediately fall apart. Alternatively, she flips her hair from side to side or ineffectually tucks it behind her ears. If all else fails, she twirls her tresses between her fingers—over and over. Sometimes Goldilocks is replaced by the knee jerker or his next of kin: the toe tapper, nail biter, facial tic-er, napkin tearer, and spoon banger. To all of them I'd like to recommend sitting on your hands or, even better, donning a pair of handcuffs. Finally, for those who repetitively pat their heads, dart out their tongue, wink their eyes, and tug on their ear (unless they're Carol Burnett), I would prescribe a strong tranquilizer. On second thought, that one's for me.

But that's only half the equation of my misery. On my left is the snuffler. There must be a special place in heaven for snufflers, and I wish they would go there, preferably before it's wheels up. Akin to the young (and sometimes old) and the restless referenced above, I am irritated by the post-nasally chal-lenged. I'm dying to say, "Didn't your mother tell you never to leave the house without a handkerchief?" Apparently not. To add insult to injury, when I offer you a Kleenex, you say, "No, thanks; I'm okay." Let me assure you that you are not okay and I am definitely not okay with your sniff, sniff, sniff routine. Dry and wet coughers, you don't get a pass, either. Is it too much to ask that you carry throat lozenges with you when you must have had this scourge for at least ten days? I heard you hocking and hacking in the waiting area before our flight was called, and now I see you're sitting next to me. Let's just say it's a good thing the windows in this plane are welded shut or one of us would be practicing our sky diving.

I'm trying to be Zen about my fellow passengers, I really am. I mean "Live and Let Live" is tattooed across my heart. But just as I say this the very last flier is making a beeline for my row, and it looks as though she's smuggled in a tiny dog under her coat. It looks like a yapper. Shouldn't someone notify the SPCA, TSA, FBI, or CIA? Next time, I swear I'm taking the train to England.

WINNING SMILE

Active grandmother with original teeth seeking dedicated flosser to share rare steaks, corn on the cob and caramel candy.

—Florida retirement complex ad

LET'S HEAR IT FOR THE RED, WHITE AND BLUE

When I say, "Let's hear it for the red, white, and blue," I am not referring to Old Glory, although I like to think I'm as patriotic as the next person. No, I am saluting those basic colors that everyone knows—or used to know. In kindergarten if not before, we learned that red means stop and green means go. But copywriters could not leave well enough alone, so they "improved" upon the names of colors until today confusion reigns. When they describe slacks as *medium saddle*, for example, those of us who have not been riding to the hounds lately do not find this helpful.

Now that we're consigned to shopping online, it's more important than ever that a color's name tell us exactly what it is since we can't eyeball the goods directly. No such luck. Part of the credit or discredit for this must go to the Color Council, an organization dedicated to the proposition that nothing in the stores this year can match anything in our closets from last year. As far as I was concerned the color wheel wasn't broke, but the powers that be felt they had to fix it, anyway. And that's why we got:

- **Blueprint:** Presumably some shade of blue, this was named the Color of the Year for 2019. Since no one has actually seen a paper blueprint since poodle skirts and Elvis Presley, this seems like a quixotic choice. I mean, will bluebirds now have to be renamed "The blueprint of happiness" and new lyrics devised for "When Sunny gets blueprint . . ."?

- **Tequila sunrise.** Not to be confused with *tequila sunset*, this red will have its challenges when it comes into everyday use. It will have to replace the standard phrase for being angry with, "I was so mad I saw tequila sunrise!" And the driving test will have to be amended to ask, "When can you not make a right turn on tequila sunrise?" As for our poor little robin of song, it would now be, "When the tequila sunrise comes bob, bob bobbing along . . ."

- ***Morrocan mint.*** Green is one of those colors the catalogue writers just can't seem to leave alone as witnessed by its many variations: kiwi, lime, avocado, emerald, celadon, chartreuse, jade, Kelly, olive, hunter, shamrock, and Hooker's (Hooker's?). While I get the allure of alliteration, I have to wonder whether with morrocan mint, are you offering me a cup of tea or okaying my new literary project? And somehow the classic movie doesn't make it as, "How Morrocan Mint was my Valley."

- ***Ultra Violet:*** This was the Color of the Year for 2018, but I personally find monikers for the color purple confusing. I mean, what's up with lavender, lilac, dahlia, orchid, plum, pomegranate, and grape? Are we planting a garden here or just trying to find a bright-looking couch to fill up a corner of the living room?

- ***Powder:*** In one color thesaurus, white has 588 synonyms. These include but are not limited to: salt, lace, cocoanut, pearl, alabaster, egg shell, chiffon, powder, porcelain, and rice. It's enough to turn your hair, well, chiffon, or was that cocoanut? I don't know about you, but this year "I'm Dreaming of an Egg Shell Christmas."

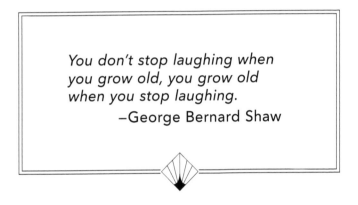

*You don't stop laughing when
you grow old, you grow old
when you stop laughing.*
    —George Bernard Shaw

CHRISTMAS AT
THE KIDS'

This time of the year there are always tons of articles for the younger generation on how to survive the holidays at their folks. Well, as someone who spent last Christmas at my grown kids' house, let me assure you that it was no bed of roses, either. Of course, I loved seeing them, and they tried hard to be gracious hosts. Still, this old body had some hurdles to overcome.

First, I had to trek 2,750 miles to that yuppie haven called Brooklyn, New York, and climb the ever-so-steep/ever-so-narrow steps up to their brownstone's teeny-weeny landing. Then I had to pray that someone inside was restraining the two Great Danes lest they hurl me back onto the sidewalk, which they had been known to do. Miraculously, I made it through the front door—narrowly avoiding the pointy antique mirror that threatened to take out my left eye—and beheld my roommates for the next six days.

There was my daughter with a strained smile on her face. There was my son-in-law, who was thrilled beyond words to give up their bed for a week. Then there were the two hyperactive preschoolers, who had been told so many times to behave when grandma visited that they were virtually vibrating. Rounding out the company were said Great Danes and a little designer dog before which the Danes cowered. That made 14 eyeballs, 20 legs, and 110 decibels of noise. Something was always prowling, wagging, barking or shrieking, which for some reason I found slightly unnerving.

Did I mention that the kids' house, while fashionable, is extremely tight? Do not let that big Brooklyn price tag fool you into thinking that a former rooming house built in 1885 must be a mega-mansion. *Au contraire*. Let's just say my daughter and her husband, who both work in the television industry—which is a very Brooklyn thing to do, by the way—have to stash their Emmy Awards among the pots and pans because their only other only shelf holds the essentials: dog food and Legos.

Not that they miss the dining space because they don't seem to eat. In my book a kale smoothie does not a meal make. No wonder hunger drove me out into the streets in search of real food. In their oh-so-hip neighborhood: chai tea cafes, maybe. Afro-Cuban-Asian-fusion restaurants, definitely. Gluten-free artisanal patisseries, *mai oui*. But anything recognizable as good old American fare, forget it. So I did and existed on Kind bars for six days.

Then there was the little matter of heat, or lack thereof. Christmastime in New York is freezing, so I climbed into bed to get warm, which the dogs seemed to think was a swell idea, too. Unfortunately, they took it upon themselves to expel a lot of noxious fumes. Catching wind of this (ha, ha) my daughter threw open the window to sweeten the air. Now I had the worst of both worlds: I was once again ice cold and I couldn't move because I was pinned down by 300 pounds of dog flesh. Little did I know that the Great Danes were accustomed to sacking out on MY bed with their heads on MY pillows. Some dogs have no respect for boundaries! Of course, from their point of view there were no boundaries; I was so covered in dog hair they thought I was one of their own.

I think I'll celebrate at home this year. Even if I fly everyone out and pay for doggie camp, it will be a bargain at twice the price.

And you thought I was making
all this stuff up . . .

ACKNOWLEDGMENTS

Many thanks to those who helped launch my so-called career as a humorist. Chief among them is Greg Dodds, who published my very first personal memoir, "Hair," in *BoomerCafe. com* and accepted every one of the pieces I sent in thereafter. Greg's encouragement gave me my first inkling that others might find me funny, too.

Alas, today there's a lot more that goes into being an author than pecking away at a keyboard. In fact, it now takes a village. That's why I'd like to pay homage to my fabulous SCORE counselor, John Richardson, who has (figuratively) held my hand every step of the way. Ditto, Cynthia Burt, website designer extraordinaire, who came up with the idea that I should become a "brand." And when it comes to designers, Chris Nolt of Cirrus Book Design is both a terrific talent and a delight to work with. Alexandra Trujillo has been great in keeping me on track with the dreaded social media.

Rounding out the list of those who have helped me get to this point are Betsy Green of the Santa Barbara Independent Writers Group, who is always generous with her time and knowledge. I'd also like to recognize those Santa Barbara organizations that give local writers a chance to be heard, Out Loud and Speaking of Stories. SOS's theatrical director, Maggie Mixsell, was skillful in teaching me how to kick it up a notch.

Finally, a tip of the hat to my supportive family members who make me laugh. I notice that they are being especially nice to me these days. I guess they're afraid that if they tick me off, I'll lampoon them in one of my stories. Could that be why my long-suffering husband, Jon—who has read and re-read every word I ever wrote—has also been on his best behavior of late? I hope he knows that no matter how much I poke fun at his idiosyncrasies, I love him madly and admire him deeply.

ABOUT THE AUTHOR

Barbara Greenleaf has a day job. She writes the bi-monthly blog, *www.ParentsOfGrownOffspring.com,* which deals with the many issues that arise in today's adult family. But she also has a side hustle, and that is writing humor. Sometimes she spends more time on the side hustle than on the day job, and the result is her latest book, *THIS OLD BODY: And 99 Other Reasons to Laugh at Life.*

Barbara began writing at the age of eight, when she composed her Last Will & Testament. After graduating from Vassar College, she worked at *The New York Times* and was granted her first book contract at the age of 24. She has seven books to her credit, including the award-winning *America Fever: The Story of American Immigration.* Her other books are *Forward March to*

Freedom, a juvenile biography of A. Philip Randolph; *Children Through the Ages: A History of Childhood*; *Help: A Handbook for Working Mothers* with Louis Schaffer, M.D.; and the young adult novels, *Animal Kingdom* and *Good-to-Go Café*. In addition, she has penned numerous articles and speeches, one of which won a Best Speech in L.A. Award and two others that were published in *Vital Speeches of the Day*. She served as a contributing editor at *Working Mother* magazine.

Over the years Barbara applied her communications and consulting skills to the corporate world. She worked for an energy conglomerate and a satellite communications firm before founding Greenleaf Video, a purveyor of nonfiction videos. After selling that company, she started Strategic Communications/LA, where her clients included the RAND Corporation, the Santa Monica Pier, and the SPCA/LA. More recently, she was

Associate Vice Chancellor of Antioch University Santa Barbara.

On the volunteer side, Barbara helped save agricultural land in Goleta, mentored students at Santa Barbara High School, and founded the Santa Barbara Jewish Film Festival. She has been married since the Civil War to the dashing Jon Greenleaf, with whom she shares two daughters and four grandchildren. When she's not blogging or kidding around about the everyday humiliations and aggravations of growing older, Barbara can be found creating mixed media art.

LET'S NOT SAY GOODBYE...

Want more humor in your life? Get your monthly fix with the **Laughter Letter**, Barbara's free gift of funny. Sign up at *www.barbaragreenleaf.com* and let the chuckles begin!

Send Barbara your funny stories, jokes, and quips to barbara@barbaragreenleaf.com. She'll post them on social media and you'll see your name in print.

If you enjoyed *THIS OLD BODY* (and even if you didn't), please take a moment to write a short review on Amazon. It will encourage other readers to see what the fuss is all about.

You can follow Barbara at:

Twitter:
https://twitter.com/bkgreenleaf

Instagram:
https://www.instagram.com/barbarathewriter/

Facebook:
https://www.facebook.com/barbara.greenleaf.71